Useful

Bits & Pieces

Biblical Monologues, Stories,
Readings & Dialogues for Easy Use
Here, There and Everywhere

Previously published as Monday Rewrites on
www.davehopwood.com

by

Dave Hopwood

Other books by Dave Hopwood:

Telling Tales
120 Interactive Bible Stories for All Ages

Top Stories
31 Biblical Parables Retold for Adults

Lyrical Riffs
A collection of short readings for use in services, meetings and personal reflection

Film & Faith
66 Film clips that bring the Bible to life

Parables
A collection of short stories to ponder and share

Jonny & The Fog
An inventive retelling of the life of Jesus, entertaining and gripping

The Groovy Gospel
An entertaining way to read the stories about Jesus (includes cartoons & quizzes)

Breaking Into the Good Book
Three strangers break into the Bible and encounter its characters, via a few wires and a glass of green smoking liquid. A novel of biblical proportions.

Dave is a freelance author and speaker, and is available for workshops, seminars and speaking engagements. www.davehopwood.com

For Martin, thanks so much for your hard work and editing on this and all the other books.

Title	Page

Title	Page

A Wise Man Wonders

Themes: Epiphany, the Wise Men, Herod
Bible Refs: Numbers 24 v 17, Matthew 2 vv 1-18

I look back on it every year around this time. And I can't help but wonder – was it our fault? Did we start it? We'd been on that road all that time. Carefully following the charts, cutting a new path, drawing on Balaam's ancient prophecy. And what did we do? Fall at the last hurdle. We were looking for a good king so we went to see a bad king instead. Some might say we weren't to know, couldn't have imagined the fallout from that visit. But we can't deny what happened.

We weren't there afterwards, didn't hear the screams or smell the blood. We were just told. Stopped by a gasping, wild-eyed messenger as we journeyed back, I remember clambering off my camel, twisting my ankle as I fell, and being sick in the road. The other two, bantering happily a second before about the new king, turned and stared back at Bethlehem, their mouths twisted and hanging open like gashed windows. No one spoke for quite a while. Eventually we rode on in silence. Herod had worn a mask of mock wonder when we visited him, swore blind he wanted to worship this new king. Promised on his mother that he would go if we just popped back and let him know the whereabouts.

We didn't pop back and we didn't tell him, and he didn't go. But he sent troops instead. And the troops brought a death wish. A killing curse. And when they'd finished children lay stone-still in the streets. The future of Bethlehem cut down. The babies' crying replaced with that of their mothers. So I wonder – what would have happened if we hadn't dropped by on the palace? If we'd stayed away from the sick, paranoid king. Would he have heard another way? Would he have perpetrated slaughter anyway? I'll never know, but I think on it each year around this time.

That was three decades ago now, but the memory lingers, like an open wound. My travelling companions died a while back, but I have heard it said that the Bethlehem baby has grown up – the one boy not cut down that night. And something is nudging me to saddle up again and pay him a visit. Perhaps there'll be some kind of healing for me in doing that... I may well go.

Counting Sheep

Themes: God's plans, family, regret
Bible Refs: Genesis 37

Jacob (reflecting):

I don't count my sheep anymore. They say I'm doing well these days. My livestock are thriving. Things go well. But I don't care. Not now. There was a time when gathering sheep and goats was a major preoccupation. Of course it was, it was everything. I did plenty of deals and fast talking in order to feather the nest. But I don't care now. Too painful to think on.

I met a man the other day. A stranger. He dropped by and we did the usual thing. Welcomed him with feasting and drinking. It was only halfway through the evening that he mentioned it. That day out at Shechem. I thought he was raising the spectre of Simeon and Levi. Even feared for a moment that he might be here on some kind of killing spree. A hired man come with belated revenge in his fist for the attack on the Shechem men. Those boys ran wild that day. Retribution they called it for Shechem's violation of their sister. But it was appalling. Not an eye for an eye. A sack full of eyes. A cartload. God knows I was broken by the attack on Dinah. But these boys knew no restraint. No shame.

But it wasn't about that. No, it seems he had another son in mind. The one always on my mind. He met him once he said. Had a chat with him. Said he seemed like a nice guy. Course he was. Not the slaughtering sort like Simeon or Levi. Or the carnal kind like Judah or Reuben. Off sleeping with women like there's no tomorrow. It was only as the conversation progressed that I realised. He hadn't just met on any day. On a day when everything was normal. On a day when the sun rose and set and life continued as usual. No. He met him… on that day. In fact… this was the thing, this was what cut deep, this was what added to the chill in my heart… he found him wandering, lost, looking for his brothers. In Shechem. Did he send him home, did he send him safely back to me? No. Not at all. He'd heard the brothers talking, knew they'd left and headed for Dothan. That Canaanite centre that Judah loves so much. Plenty of water and amenities there. Plenty of women no doubt too.

Why? Why did he have to tell me about it now? Why did he have to do it in the first place? This stupid interfering stranger. If he hadn't bumped into Joe that day, if he hadn't overheard the other boys, if he hadn't gone out of his way to tell Joe where they were… he'd be alive. My boy. Rachel's son. He'd still be here. Wouldn't he? Still grinning and warming my heart and going on and on about his dreams. Wouldn't have got attacked and killed. I wouldn't be sitting here now with that bloody coat of his in that dark corner.

It was odd when he left. That stranger. Didn't so much walk off into the distance. He started walking but then there was a strange kind of shimmering. He sort of faded. Long before I'd have expected him to disappear from my sight. He was just gone. Almost like… well I saw angels in a dream once. Going up and down between heaven and earth. He wasn't quite like that, and yet, I couldn't help wondering. He guided Joe, like they guided me. I wrestled with an angel once too. All night. Now this stranger was more like that. He smiled as he went, told me the story wasn't finished. What did that mean? Not finished? And something about what was intended for harm being turned to good. Those were his final words. Confusing.

I don't count my sheep anymore. I can't. Because I sent Joe to do it that day. Sent him to check on his wayward brothers and make sure my property was being looked after. And it got him killed. If only I…

I can't worry about sheep any more.

The Josiah Kyle Show

Themes: The virgin birth, Christmas
Bible Refs: Luke 1 vv 26-38, Matthew 1 vv 18-25

TV Host Josiah Kyle walks on, suited, suave and confidently brash.

JOS. Today on the Josiah Kyle show we have a young couple in dire straits. Young Joe is worried, let me tell you. He's been hearing rumours round the town. Rumours about his fiancée Mary. Let's bring them on and see if there's any truth in the gossip. Ladies and gentlemen, a big hand for Mary and Joe. (Applause as they enter and take a seat)

JOS. Now, Mary, you claim that you have never even kissed another man?

MAR. That's right.

JOS. And you've never been intimate with another man?

MAR. That's right.

JOS. In fact, you claim you've never kissed any man. At all. Ever. Not even Joe here.

MAR. That's right.

JOS. Hmm. (Thinks) And yet you Mary… and correct me if I'm wrong here… you say you've never even kissed a man and yet Mary – you're pregnant!

(Gasps from the audience)

JOS. That's right ladies and gents. This woman, who claims to be as pure as the driven snow, is with child!

MAR. How d'you know? Who told you?

JOS. Your cousin told us, she was only too happy to talk about your... situation. She's excited about it. Well, she's pregnant herself. We had her on the show last week, after her husband was so shocked about their pregnancy that he was struck dumb. She wasn't though. She was very chatty, and your name came up. So, do you still claim you haven't slept with someone?

MAR. Yes. Absolutely.

JOS. Even though the newspapers claim different?

MAR. Absolutely.

JOS. Even though your neighbours, many of them here in the audience, tell us otherwise?

MAR. Yes.

JOS. So it must be Joseph's baby then?

MAR. No.

JOS. But if you haven't been with anyone else... look, make it easy on yourself. Wouldn't it be better just to say that it is Joseph's? He seems a nice enough chap. What have you got against him?

MAR. Nothing, I want to marry him. I love him.

JOS. Is he not good enough for you? Are you after someone richer?

MAR. No!

JOS. Someone cooler? Funnier? Better Looking?

MAR. No!

JOS. But... and again, correct me if I'm wrong... ladies and gentlemen he's only gone and broken off the engagement.

(More gasps from the audience)

JOE. No I haven't. I'm still thinking about it.

JOS. All right. Well, you both took a lie detector test earlier. How d'you think it'll turn out Mary?

MAR. I'm telling the truth.

JOS. Joe, what do you think?

JOE. I don't know what to think.

JOS. Well let's see, I have the results in this envelope here. (He opens it.) Mary have you picked a name for the baby?

MAR. Yes. Jesus.

JOS. And if it's a girl?

MAR. It's a boy.

JOS. How can you be so sure? Have you had a scan?

MAR. No. I had a message. From an angel.

JOS. An angel! Oh this gets better and better. And what about poor Joe? He doesn't get an angel.

JOE. Actually... I did.

JOS. You saw an angel too?

JOE. I had a dream. That's why I've decided. I've made up my mind now. I'm not breaking off the engagement.

(More gasps from the audience)

JOS. Well, Joe, I can tell you this... (looks at the card) the results of the lie detector test... confirm that Mary is... telling the truth! (Even more gasps) Yes ladies and gentlemen, that's what this show is all about. Getting to the truth! So you heard it first here. Mary hasn't had any other relationships and yet somehow – she's pregnant. Must be some kind of miracle. See you tomorrow when we'll be meeting three very wise men, who claim they've seen a message in the stars about a whole new king. Join me and find out all about it.

End with the sound of audience applause.

Nativity Tableau

Themes: Christmas, Jesus
Bible Refs: Luke 2 vv 1-20

Cast: Stage Manager (SM); Flo & Doris (two cleaners); Innkeeper (IK) & Wife; 2 Rats; 3 Kings; 3 Shepherds; Dog and Donkey; Mary and Joseph

SM.   Right you lot get into position – we need the shepherds, kings, Mary, Joseph, donkey, sheep, dog, rats, innkeeper and his wife.

(The cast make an awkward tableau)

SM.   Good – that should be okay. Nice traditional picture. The real meaning of it all. That's what Christmas is all about. Flo and Doris – you can't be in the picture.

Flo.   They might have had a couple of cleaners. I mean it would have been dirty in that stable.

Doris. It would have been filthy – full of cockroaches and scorpions and things.

SM.   Don't be ridiculous. There would not have been cleaners in the stable.

IK.   There wouldn't have been an innkeeper either.

SM. What?

IK. There's no innkeeper in the Bible. It's a nice idea but he's not mentioned.

Flo. See! If the innkeeper's allowed in then we're staying.

SM. All right then.

Doris. We can stay?

SM. NO. You're all out. Flo, Doris and the Innkeeper.

IK. But it's the only bit I'm doing. I've told my kids I've got a big part.

SM. Sorry. Off you go.

IK. Well, the wife can't stay then.

SM. What?

IK. The innkeeper's wife – if there wasn't an innkeeper he wouldn't have had a wife. Lucky fella…

Voice (off stage) I heard that!

SM. All right. Innkeeper's wife, sorry Petunia, you're out.

IKW. Ooh good, I can get home and watch *White Christmas*…

Rat1. Can we go too then?

SM. Why?

Rat2. Well we don't look like rats – we're too big.

Rat1. We look like mutant rats. We're massive.

Rat2. We must have been eating GM crop leftovers.

SM.   All right – you do look a bit stupid.

Rat1. No we don't. You look stupid.

IK.   There wouldn't have been any kings either.

SM.   Are you still here?

IK.   They were actually wise men – but they didn't get there till two years later.

SM.   (Sighs) Right! Kings – you're fired.

Kings. Ooooh!

       (Donkey starts to leave too)

SM.   Where are you going?

Donk. I don't want to be a donkey.

Dog.   Can I be a donkey – I don't want to be a dog.

Donk. Can I be a dog then? We'll swap.

SM.   No one's swapping!

Sh1.   Actually I don't think the shepherds had sheepdogs then.

SM.   Right! All the animals out! Now! All of you… Dogs, cats, rats, bats, sheep, horses, cows, wolves, llamas, badgers, ferrets, guinea pigs, gerbils, mice…

Sh1. There probably would have been some mice…

SM   Shut up! Right! We should be left with Mary, Joseph and the shepherds. Anyone else got any complaints?

IK.   Actually – some people think it wasn't in a stable at all.

SM. Are you still here?

IK.   Joseph would have been well known in his home town, they're very big on hospitality in that part of the world. It's unlikely he'd have been left out in the cold.

SM.   You'll be out in the cold if you don't be quiet. (Shepherds start to leave) Where are you going?

Sh1. We've got football practice. We're playing the Baptists on Boxing Day and they're vicious.

SM.   I'll be vicious in a min… oh….

      (Everyone drifts off just leaving Mary and Joe, SM buries his head in his hands, then looks up again, when everyone's gone)

SM.   You're still here then? You haven't got a
       good reason to flee the stable?

       (They shake their heads)

SM.   Mary and Joseph and a baby – not much
       of a Christmas tableau is it?

Mary. No – but it is the best bit.

SM.   Yea – I suppose it is.

They freeze for a moment then all get up and
leave.

Peace On Earth?

Themes: Conflict, Peace, Gossip, Criticism
Bible Refs: Ephesians 4 v 32, John 15 vv 9-14

A little festive reading/sketch for a narrator (N) and a group of readers. There are 9 readers here (1-9), but you could do it with less.

N. Right. Drama group – up you come. Let's practice the Peace on Earth reading. Come on.

The group walk on and start reading.

1. Christmas is a time for peace

2. It's a time for harmony

3. A time for caring and coming together as one.

4. For a son is born to us, and he will be called The Prince of Peace

5. His ever-expanding reign will be one of reconciliation and peace.

6. Wild animals will lie down together, children will play with snakes.

7. Everyone will live in harmony and safety.

8. Peace will be the watchword of the day

9. And harsh words will never again be heard in the land.

N. Great. That's perfect.

1. Well I was all right – but she's too quiet.

2. No I'm not – you speak too fast.

3. She does not! If anyone's got a problem it's you.

4. Shut up! Stop going on at her.

5. Don't tell her to shut up!

6. Yea, or we'll both shut you up.

7. Don't make me laugh – you couldn't shut anyone up.

8. Stop arguing you lot.

9. Yea – stop going on at each other!

All.   We're not arguing!

8&9. Yes you are.

All.   Oh no we're not.

8&9. Oh yes you are!

All.   Oh no we're not.

8&9. Oh yes you are! (etc.)

N.   All right – let's stop being childish.

All.   We are not being childish!

N.   Be quiet!

All.   (Mimicking) Be quiet!

N.   All right – let's move on.

All.   (Mimicking) All right! Let's move on.

They walk off still arguing.

A Bit Shepherdist?

Themes: Jesus is approachable and available
Bible Refs: Luke 2 vv 8-20, John 1 v 14

Two people (1&2) enter caught up in the following conversation.

1. Three shepherds walked into a building, you'd have thought at least one of them would have seen it coming.

2. That's not funny.

1. All right, how about this one? Never call a first-century shepherd on the phone when he's doing the ironing.

2. That's not funny either. In fact it sounds a bit shepherdist to me.

1. All right – how d'you sink a submarine full of shepherds? Knock on the door. Get it? Knock on the door!

2. First-century shepherds didn't have submarines! Or irons!… Or phones!!

1. All right then, how about this, three first-century shepherds saw a choir of angels in the sky and then found a baby in an animal trough.

2. Again – that's not funny!

1. Well… depends on your point of view. Probably sounded funny to a first-century night club audience.

2. What?

1. They were the butt of the jokes. Shepherds. The community target. They didn't smell great because they slept with the sheep, and couldn't keep pace with all the religious laws. They were the last people on earth you'd have expected to be told about the birth of God's son. But look what happened. Huge choir of angels, big speech from one of the big-winged guys about a saviour and goodwill and peace on earth, and then – voom!

2. Voom?

1. Voom!! Straight down to Bethlehem and there he is, the promised new baby. Easily identifiable because he's in an animal trough and – more importantly – approachable by a bunch of people who everyone else looks down on. They'd have felt right at home meeting a new king in an animal trough. Sort of place they regularly hung around.

2. Wow!

1. Indeed wow! And that was just the start. It was the template for the rest of his life. A new kind of king – born in a lowly place, no palace or paparazzi or servants. It set the scene for the rest

of his time, for meeting ordinary and marginalised people.

2. Incredible.

1. Quite.

2. Just one thing though.

1. What now?

2. They don't have wings.

1. Who – shepherds?

2. No. Angels. They don't have wings. You said 'the big-winged guy'. No wings.

1. Not even small ones?

2. Not even tiny.

1. What about shepherds?

2. Well, they probably ran around the town like they'd been on Red Bull all night after seeing the new baby. And they say that gives you wiiings.

1. True. (pause) Are you being sponsored by Red Bull for this dialogue?

They freeze for a moment then leave.

Freddy Function Bucks The Trend

Themes: Going against the flow, being countercultural, choosing to be different
Bible Refs: Ephesians 2 v 10, Romans 12 v 2

Freddy Function refused to toe the line. At school he was always in trouble for turning up late, working too slowly, asking the wrong questions and making unexpected comments.

At church he sat down when others stood up, stood up when others sat down, sang the hymns at the wrong speed and often interrupted the well-prepared sermons.

He was never cool, always behind the times and not much interested in the latest trends. But he was often there in a crisis, or hanging around when someone needed a smile. His words were not the most eloquent but they spurred others on to a more hopeful day and a kind of small greatness.

He didn't much bother about *Keep off the grass* signs if there was a good reason to get from a to b. And there often was. He spoke too loudly in the library and laughed at jokes no one else got. But he was always there to volunteer when the crowd dispersed.

His hands were rarely clean but that was because he was not afraid to get them dirty. He'd heard about the Health and Safety Regulations, but then he'd heard about *50 Shades of Grey* too, and hadn't taken much notice of that either.

He was bound to get into trouble, and frequently upset people, but the number of those he encouraged was greater.

Eventually, when those with more power than Freddie got fed up of his holy shenanigans, they arrested him on a trumped up charge, engineered a smear campaign, stirred up dissent and disposed of him.

Not surprising really, he wasn't the first to be crucified for this sort of thing.

The Meeting

Themes: Power and weakness
Bible Refs: John 19 vv 8-11, 1 Corinthians 1 v 25

Imagine if Pilate and Jesus had met a week before their conversation on Good Friday.

Pilate. (pushing through the crowd) Outa my way, outa my way... keep back there, keep back. Ah! There he is. Jesus, just the man. Now listen to me. I'm telling you, listen. I've got a show to run here. And it ain't an easy job. I've heard about you and I know what the people say, and I just want to make sure you know this – don't cross me. Don't make life difficult for yourself or for me. You may think you have power, but trust me – you have no idea. When it comes to Rome – we know what power is, we invented it, and we serve it up and we dish it out when the time is right. If you and I cross swords, if we meet on a dark night, and you come making trouble, trust me, one of us is going down, and it won't be me. I mean you no harm, I have nothing against you. But I have to keep this moth-eaten ship afloat here. Trust me, running this backwoods country is no walk in the park. I have to hold the thing tightly by the scruff of the neck. So it's no use coming with your miracles and your divine talk of power and glory. I am the power and glory round here. So let's not get any wires crossed. You understand?

(Jesus crouches down and draws on a piece of paper.)

Pilate. What? What are you doing? What is that? Are you listening to me? Are you taking heed? Am I wasting my breath here?

(Jesus looks up. Smiles. Nods. Thinks for a moment then draws on the paper again)

Pilate. You know, I'm a reasonable man. I have family, a wife, servants, pets. I entertain all kinds of people. I go dancing, walking, climbing, I'm not a barbarian. I'm a civilised man. I'm not a tyrant. I want a peaceful outcome here. I'm not looking for a fight. But I have a king to serve. And I will serve him. That's why I'm here now. I want to avoid harm and bloodshed. I don't want to find myself called from my bed in the dark hours to oversee another crucifixion. You wouldn't want that, would you?

Jesus. (looking up at Pilate) I know of your power, Pilate, I understand it, and I care about it, but it doesn't come from your king. Can I tell you a story? There was a master, with two servants. And he sent the two men off into the world with a mission. The first came riding on a stallion, wielding power and influence, surrounded by gleaming soldiers. The other came humbly, riding on a donkey, walking with beggars and outcasts and prostitutes. The two men completed their missions, one triumphing, the other dying. However, in triumphing the first lost everything, whilst in dying the second gained all. The first knew the weakness of power, whilst the second knew the power of weakness. D'you understand?

Pilate. Understand what? What are you talking about? Power? Yes, I know about power, I told you. Weakness? The first, the second, two servants… a master… who are you talking about? It's just confusing. They told me you do this. Tell these stories

which only confound and mystify. Jesus
I'm warning you, stay in line. D'you hear
me? Stay in line. Don't rock the boat or
you will pay the price. I promise you that.

Pilate storms off. Jesus finishes drawing on the
paper, stands and pins it up. He has drawn three
crosses on a hill and the outline of a man
washing his hands. (This picture could be
prepared beforehand, and Jesus would then just
mime drawing during the sketch.)

Jesus leaves.

Locked

Themes: The God who reaches out to us
Bible Refs: Hebrews 4 vv 14-16, John 3 v 16

Imagine if the gates of heaven were locked

If truth were cloudy and distorted

And the world had leaked all purpose and hope.

Imagine if the way to Life was not wide or narrow

But impossibly blocked with fallen debris

A permanent *Road Closed* sign sealing the way.

Imagine if the author of life had run out of ink

If the divine imagination had stopped creating

And we lived and moved and existed in a void.

Imagine if all humour were cynical and hollow

If the source of compassion dried up

And all good nature were turning steadily sour.

Imagine if we were cut adrift

If we were all stranded on a dying desert island

And there was no one greater than frail humans.

Imagine if an angel had rescued the son of man in the Garden of Gethsemane

If the cup of suffering had been left for another day

And a lowly carpenter had not died on that cross.

Imagine if the work of redemption had remained unfinished

If Calvary had only held two crosses, not three.

Imagine if the dying thief had called out 'Remember me…'

And there had been no response.

Now imagine something else.

Not Fair

For a group sketch version of this see page 157.

Themes: The parable of the workers, God's mercy, God's ways
Bible Refs: Matthew 20 vv 1-15, Matthew 7 v 24 and Luke 23 vv 39-43

Once there was a woman who decided to build her own house. She knew nothing about building houses but she thought it couldn't be that difficult, so she bought a nice plot of land and started to dig. However, she made a big mistake, she built the house very quickly and on a swamp with no foundations. And while she was asleep it collapsed and fell on top of her. She woke to find bits of the ceiling in her mouth and the toilet nowhere in sight.

So she decided to try again, this time she bought a bit of land that was good and solid, and this time she decided to get some help. So she went into the nearby town and found some people sitting around on the bench in the town square.

'I want some help to build my house,' she said. 'I want it done properly with good foundations and a nice little fountain in the garden.'

But the people seemed reluctant to help. So she scratched her head, had a think and then said, 'I'll pay you all £200 if you'll help me.' Suddenly – they weren't so busy, and they leapt up, signed a contract and started work on the house.

At coffee time she went into town to buy some doughnuts for everyone and she spotted a large group of people on the bench in the town square. She asked them if they wanted to earn a few quid. They all leapt up and she had to buy twice as many doughnuts. At lunchtime the woman went into town to buy some veggie burgers. She spotted some more people in the town square. She asked them if they wanted to help her build a house. And so they leapt up and helped her carry the veggie burgers back to the building site. At teatime she went in for some cream cakes and saw another crowd in the town square. A group of workers that nobody else would hire. So she asked them if they wanted to help her as well. By the time they'd finished work the building site was full of weary workers and empty food bags.

The woman said, 'Come and collect your wages.'

The teatime recruits lined up first and the woman paid them each £200.

'Excellent!' said the lunchtime recruits, 'we'll get twice as much.'

'Cool!' said the coffee time recruits. 'We'll get three times as much!'

'Even better,' said the morning recruits, 'we'll get four times as much.'

But they didn't, they all got £200. There was nearly a riot.

'It's not fair,' they said. 'We've worked all day and only got the same as the people who just did a bit at the end.'

'Oh dear,' said the woman, 'I must have made a mistake.' And she scratched her head and looked confused. So the woman took out their contracts and had a look.

'No, that's right,' she said. 'Look, you agreed to work all day for £200. It says so here.'

'Yes, but that's not fair…' they said.

But the woman shook her head and said, 'There's no mistake. It's my money, if I want to be generous that's up to me. There's no need for you to get jealous about it.'

Some of the workers went away grumpily, thought about this, and changed their minds. But others grew increasingly angry and never helped the woman again. Still others are still chewing on it and considering what to do…

A Woman's Place

Themes: Jesus is countercultural, Mary and Martha, Jesus and equality
Bible Refs: Luke 10: 38-42

Jesus has the wrong sort of hands. Builder's hands. Not rabbi's. There isn't a religious teacher in Israel walking around with those gnarled knuckles and cracked fingers. Carpenters don't become rabbis. This guy looks like a cowboy. Going around changing the rules and flouting the law, and teaching other people to do the same. That can't be right. His whole being is wrong. He doesn't look noble enough, doesn't look noble at all. It's all wrong. Fishermen don't become disciples. Toll collectors don't. Freedom fighters don't. And women. Certainly not women.

'Jesus, I want a word.' She hisses her demand at him.

Jesus sighs, straightens his robe and stands. She beckons and takes him outside.

'This isn't right. You know that don't you? There's already talk, you make matters worse like this.'

'What kind of talk?'

'You know. About you and the women you spend time with. You'll lose all respect. I'm serious. No wonder the authorities won't take you seriously, you're always crossing boundaries. They think you're a false prophet and you know what Moses said, false prophets must be stoned.'

'Martha, what's behind this?'

'What d'you mean?'

'This isn't just concern for my reputation. Is it your sister?'

Martha purses her lips. Her face hardens, those lines on her brow furrow, those deep brown eyes narrow.

He smooths a hand across her forehead. She snatches her head away, glances around.

'Stop it! That's what I mean. What will people think?'

'People will think what they want to think. What's bothering you about Mary?'

'Tell her she's in the wrong place. She shouldn't be in that room with you men. Tell her she should be out the back with me preparing the food. I've seen her, and I've seen the way Thomas looks at her. And John. And he's only young. You shouldn't put temptation in his way like this. It's naïve of you.'

Jesus's eyes widen. 'Naïve?'

She blushes.

'You promise too much,' she says. 'She thinks she can be a disciple. It can only end disastrously. Look at her now, look, arguing with the men, acting like one of them. It's ridiculous.'

'You're wrong, Martha, she doesn't want to be a disciple.'

Martha snorts at him, her face still flushed.

'You haven't heard her, when you're not around she says dangerous things. She's too cocky Jesus, you're leading her up a dangerous path. She thinks she can be one of the boys.'

'No, she thinks she can be one of the men.'

'What d'you mean?'

'She wants to be a rabbi, Martha, that's why she's sitting there soaking everything up. She wants to be a teacher.'

Plan A

Themes: God has chosen us to be part of his work, even though we are flawed and fragile
Bible Refs: Matthew 5 v 14, 2 Corinthians 4 v 5-7

A group of five angels wander in and look a little bored. Then Michael, the chief angel, walks on with a clipboard and addresses them. Michael's words are in bold.

M.   Right you lot – pay attention.

(They look at him)

M.   Now – I've assembled you here today as we have a problem on earth. We need to enlist some help to change the world. Now we have come up with a rather risky plan – anyone guess what it might be?

(They all scratch their heads and looked confused)

M.   Come on – you must have some ideas.

Ang 1.How about we get some superheroes.

Ang 2.Yes – like Spiderman, Superman and Batman.

Ang 3.Yes and Batgirl, Superwoman and Lara Croft.

Ang 4.Yes and Scooby Doo and Hong Kong Phooey and Dangermouse.

Ang 5.And don't forget Sproutman, Supersmelly Skunkwoman and Rhubarb girl.

M.   You're making them up now.

Ang 5.Am not! There's also the Cow Dung Kid, Bicycle Repairman and Chubby Bunny. They'll save the world.

M.   No they won't.

All.   Oh yes they will!

M.   Oh no they won't.

All.   Oh yes they will!

M.   Oh no they won't.

All.   Oh yes they will!

M.   No they won't. And be quiet. I'm in charge.

All.   Oh no you're not.

M.   Oh yes I am! Now be quiet and listen! The superheroes can't do it, they're either far too busy or you're just making them up! We need real people to make a difference.

All.   What? Like… ordinary people?

M.   Absolutely. Ordinary people.

All.   Ugh!!!

Ang 1. That'll never work.

M.   Yes it will. We'll get lots of people together and give them God's power.

All.   Oooh! (worried)

Ang 2. That sounds dangerous.

Ang 3. Some of them'll misuse it.

Ang 4. Some of them won't understand it.

Ang 5. Some of them will make lots of mistakes.

M.   No. They'll all make lots of mistakes. But it's been decided. They'll get special power to help the poor, the hurting, the prisoners, the sick, the lonely… and to generally light up the world.

Ang 1. (unimpressed) Rrrrrrright… And what's plan B?

M.   No plan B. That's all there is.

Ang 2. That's a crazy idea – who thought of that?

M.   God.

Ang 2. Oh! Right! Brilliant idea! Couldn't have done better myself.

M.   Glad you think so. 'Cause it's already been implemented. Come on, let's see how it's going…

All wander off.

If You Want A Job Doing…

Themes: Listening to others, delegation
Bible Refs: Exodus 18:13-27

Moses has a straight talking father-in-law. Jethro's about to pay him a visit in the desert and if his daughter's anything to go by then he's very probably a no-nonsense kind of guy. Well, here he is, knocking on the tent flap and asking to see the guy in charge.

'Hey Mo, how's it going?'

'Well, apart from nearly being slaughtered, then nearly drowning and now nearly starving – we're doing really well. And don't call me Mo. I'm supposed to be respected round here.'

'So I heard Mo, is that why you've got a long line of moaners outside your tent?'

'Yea, and it looks like you jumped the queue, they won't be happy.'

And as if on cue a face appears through the gap in the tent.

'He jumped the queue.'

'He's family! Respect my family!'

The face disappears, Jethro slaps Moses on the shoulder.

'Mo, take a break. Take a walk. Come on, we can slip out the back.'

Leadership's tough. Especially if you've not commanded an entire nation before.

'They look to me for everything," says Moses. 'I didn't ask for this.'

'Yea, but natural leadership just leaks out. If it's in there the dogs come sniffing around you. These people know you have the clout. You've got the aroma of the Big Man about you, Mo.'

'Well it's too much.'

'Too right, it's too much,' says Jethro. 'Back off. Delegate!'

'I can't! I'm the leader.'

'That's not what I heard. I heard it was you and Aaron.'

Moses frowns. 'I know, I asked for that initially. But if you want something doing…'

'Sure, do it yourself. And die before thirty.'

'Well that's unlikely. I'm 81.'

'Mo, listen. You're not the only leader round here. There are hundreds, and if you don't use them pretty soon they'll get bored. And then there'll be trouble, 'cause if you ain't got time to see everyone, everyone'll start looking to the other leaders. So bring 'em all in to your net. Get all the bosses together, brief 'em, oversee 'em and let them do what they're good at. Don't try and do it all. You should oversee your generals. No one else. Let the leaders deal with the man on the street, or on the sand in your case. Trust me, I know what I'm saying.'

'Jethro – give me a break.'

'I am giving you a break. It's exactly what I'm giving you.'

Moses is left pondering. Once again humility comes knocking. He must dig deep, listen to the voice of God coming at him through his father-in-law. He wants to do things his way. But he senses God at work here. He bites his lip, and bites the bullet…

The Ice Cream Man

Themes: A parable about sharing the goodness of God
Bible Refs: Proverbs 25 v 25, Isaiah 55 v 1, John 10 v 10

A man moved to a new town and bought an old run-down ice cream parlour. He figured that the spectrum of flavours he could offer would enhance people's lives no end. He revamped the place, throwing out all the old equipment. Put in brand new top-of-the-range gear and redecorated the whole place in warm appealing colours. He bought new chairs and tables, positioned a massive plastic cornet outside, and hired an assistant to help him with the rush.

There was no rush. No one came.

So he put adverts in the local paper, and posters around the town. No one came.

He got his assistant to walk up and down the high street wearing a sandwich board listing all the flavours. He created new, innovative, enticing flavours and got his assistant to stand on the corner shouting about the wonders of his new ice creams. He offered evenings of free-tasting.

No one came.

The man began to run out of money and had to let his assistant go. Only temporarily. He hoped. But as the days went by and the shop lost more money it looked increasingly as if he would have to sell up. One bleak Monday he was so depressed he went into his shop, and stood staring out of the brightly decorated window. As he watched the people pass by he spotted his assistant, looking depressed, on his way to the job centre. He felt sorry for him, so he made the biggest ice cream he could carry, went outside, and gave it to his assistant, who then sat on a nearby bench sadly eating it.

As they passed by one or two people threw him a glance.

What the man did not know was this. Ice cream had a bad name in that town. Rumours had been around for years that the parlour was a dangerous place. In the past the owners had been unkind, inconsiderate, hurtful people, and ice cream was something that could only bring bad news.

The following day the man made another ice cream, using his best flavours, and once again, he spotted his assistant passing by, his heart in his boots. So he gave him the ice cream and the assistant sat outside and ate his way through it. More people noticed him that day.

On the third day of doing this a teenager stopped and asked the assistant what he was eating. The owner came out and told her and offered a free ice cream. She said she'd think about it. Two days went by. Then she came back with a friend and for the first time the man had customers.

A week went by. The assistant continued eating a daily ice cream on a bench outside the shop. More and more people took notice, and a few of them came inside. Some even bought ice creams. The servings were generous and the customers went away satisfied. The man rehired his assistant. The days passed and more people came in, some went away intent on spreading negative rumours and gossip. But others were impressed and told others. The news spread about the new flavours on offer and before long people came from nearby towns to try them out. Gradually more and more people visited the ice cream parlour, and the folks who came were amazed at the owner's skill, creativity and generosity. Many others tried to deter folks from trying the ice cream, but against the odds, the ice cream parlour flourished.

Free Fish

Themes: The feeding of the 5000
Bible Refs: Mark 6 vv 30-44

It was the big fisherman, looking as gruff as ever. He held out his massive hand and it cupped a wedge of bread and some fish. I took it. It wasn't the way I'd cook fish but it was all right.

'Make the most of it,' he growled, 'there won't be plenty more where that came from.'

'Really?'

'No. Not if we're supposed to feed this shambles.' He waved a hand towards the crowd, showering crumbs as he did so. He moved on, reaching into a basket and pulling out another fistful. I watched him for a while then another voice brought me back to reality. Or rather, this unreal reality I was currently experiencing.

'Here.'

Another handful of bread and fish came my way. It was the young guy. John. He smiled.

'Oh no, it's okay,' I said. 'I already had some from the big guy, and I know you're short.'

'What d'you mean?'

'I know you haven't got enough for everyone.'

He threw back his head and laughed, a roaring, face-reddening laugh.

'You're joking. We'll never run out. Look.'

He showed me his basket, it was full to the brim.

'Started off with a child's supply of lunch, ended up with this banquet,' he said. 'And you know the best bit?' He indicated the crowd, and managed to do it without showering crumbs. 'This lot would never normally get to eat together. Not allowed to, see. Rich and poor, priests and prostitutes, sinners and saints. They're segregated. They don't allow it normally. But he's pulled a fast one, suddenly turned it into a picnic. Brought everyone together. Anyone's welcome. Here. You can have thirds as well if you hang around long enough.'

He shoved his food at me and I could do nothing else but take it.

I heard a grunt and a sigh and I swear the ground shook a little as the big fisherman dropped beside me. He smelt of fish and sweat, he was that close I got it immediately. He was staring at his open hands. There was more fish and bread in there.

'Look,' I said, 'it's really generous of you guys but I can't eat anymore…'

'How does he do it?' he said. 'How's he make it happen? How? How?'

He raised his gaze from his hands and stared at me. His eyes were bloodshot and dark-ringed. He was not having the best of days.

'You should eat some of it, you look hungry,' I said, clutching at straws.

'I've no appetite,' he said, 'I work all hours of the night for this stuff.'

He held up a fish tail, it wilted quickly in his fingers.

'He just makes it happen, just like that.' He looked off into the distance. 'It's the wedding all over again.'

'Cana?' I said, as a bell rang in my head.

He nodded and looked back at me. 'You were there too then? I don't recognise you, but no matter. You heard? Six jars of water into wine. Like that.' He snapped those colossal fingers of his and the fish tail flew from his hand and landed on the arm of a boy a couple of feet away. I reached over and brushed it off, the boy stared at me and scowled.

'And you know what?' the big guy went on, 'he hardly drank any of it himself. Made it for everyone else. And, made it so the groom wouldn't look a total jerk. D'you think he's the deal?'

'The deal?'

'Yea. The Messiah. The one. You see, he isn't the way I was told. He doesn't hatch plans or give rousing speeches or curry favour with the right sort of people. If you were going to plot a revolution you'd do all that wouldn't you? He just does things like this. Make fish and bread. You know, when he met me he gave me a massive catch of fish. Free. Any other rabbi would have kept it for himself. But not him. He says it's so we don't have to worry about fishing for a while, so we can do some learning.'

Taken from *Breaking Into The Good Book* by Dave Hopwood.

At Last – Song of Songs Explained!

Themes: A lighthearted take on the book of *Song of Songs*
Bible Refs: Song of Songs 7 and 9

Many Christians are embarrassed about the presence of Song of Songs in the Bible, featuring as it does, so many earthy references. But fear not, Erasmus Perfifola the third has cracked Solomon's code.

Erasmus says, 'Just substitute the words drummer in place of vine, worship group's mouths in place of blossoms and extended time of praise in place of pomegranates and it all makes sense and is a lot less embarrassing to read aloud in worship. So chapter 7 verse 12: "Let us see whether the vines have budded, whether the blossoms have opened, and whether the pomegranates are in flower…" now reads, "Let us see whether the drummer is sufficiently muffled behind six inch thick perspex, whether the worship group's mouths are opening at the right time and in tune with each other, and whether the extended praise time is geeing people up enough." You see, a lot more Christian and makes much more sense,' says Erasmus.

He continues, 'Likewise substitute hymn books for rounded thighs, PowerPoint presentation for navel, and this week's sound person for belly and chapter 9 verses 1-3 changes from, "Your rounded thighs are like jewels, the work of a skilled craftsman. Your navel is as delicious as a goblet filled with wine. Your belly is lovely, like a heap of wheat set about with lilies…" and now becomes, "Your news sheets are really well printed and the print is not too smudged, some of it is even readable. Your PowerPoint presentation is impressive and not too swirly. This week's sound and visuals person is doing a great job, and even at times is bringing up the right words to the right songs at the right times." Apply this principle to the whole of Song of Songs and it becomes a dissertation on the rights and wrongs of 21st Century church worship and really has absolutely nothing to do with sex whatsoever. Though I've yet to find a substitute for the word breasts.'

So says Erasmus Perfifola the third, who will be speaking next month on the subject of No sex please we're Christians at Spring Wine and Lee House.

Taken from the satirical one and only edition of Halo! Magazine available via email from this website.

Found! St Paul's Lost Letter

Themes: A satirical piece about the destructive power of gossip and negative attitudes
Bible Refs: 1 Corinthians 13

Archaeologists have recently made a startling and enlightening discovery. They have come across Paul's 3rd letter to the Corinthians. It was found by accident in a dilapidated church vestry by adventurer and archaeologist Bognor Brown, when he was looking for a paperclip in the back of the vicar's drawer. Previously Bognor Brown has been famous for tracking down the Holy Grail in a pub in Whitby and Noah's Ark in a boat show on the Isle of Sheppy. Brown let us cast a curious eye over Paul's long lost missive, which was scrawled on the back of three first-century beer mats and reads as follows.

[1]Hello you old Corinthians, hope you're all hunky dory and feeling groovy. [2]Thought I'd try writing this time on these little cardboard squares, they're cheaper than parchment and might help me to keep this third letter a bit shorter. [3]I got wind that some of you found 16 chapters quite a lot to get your head around over the toast and Nutella first thing in the morning. [4]Well then, straight to the point. Disregard my first two letters, I was only joking.

[5]Ah gotcha! Not really. But I do want to address some really serious issues in this third epistle. Now that the churches are getting established and really getting stuck into tearing each other apart I hope I can help. [6]You see, what really matters is the pews, the carpets, the PCC, the choir robes, and the after service tea. I mean who cares about all those lost souls dying out there when you can have a good old ding dong about the fabric of the building. [7]Not to mention spreading rumours about one another. So I advise you keep the services relatively short so you can gather as much gossip as possible afterwards. [8]When you meet, one will sing, another will teach, another will tell some special revelation but everything that's done must be useful and short short short. [9]No more than two or three should speak and someone must be ready to shout them down if it looks like they're cutting into the after-church gossip time. [10]Gossip is impatient and nasty, it is jealous, boastful and proud. It demands its own way, is irritable and very good at keeping a record of everybody else's wrongs. [11]Gossip thrives on injustice and falters when truth rears its ugly head. [12]Three things endure, faith, hope and love. But gossip can have a jolly good go at trumping them all! So don't give in. [13]Oh oh, looks like I'm running out of space so I'll say bye

for now, toodle pip, wish you were here and RSVP. Ciau. [14]St P.

Fotoshoppe Your Faith

Themes: Being honest about life and faith
Bible Refs: 2 Corinthians 12 v 9

Is your faith looking pale, patchy and colourless?

Are you tired of all those glitches in your belief system?

Annoyed every time your theology crashes?

Well, don't despair! You can now tart it up with the latest version of Fotoshoppe Your Faith!

This new version 10 contains top tools for making your faith look tidy and shiny and a whole lot better than it really might be. Sharpen up any blurred doctrine. Remove any unwanted red eye of annoyance/fury. Cut and paste some victorious Christian living into your testimony. Enhance your entire outward faith-appearance, making it appear dynamic and vibrant.

New Version 10 of Fotoshoppe Your Faith is guaranteed to:

1. Cherry pick the high points, and give the good moments an extra polished happy clappy appearance

2. Helpfully delete the worst moments and recycle the dodgy ones into examples of glorious born-again living

3. Include a dictionary of useful words and phrases like victorious, triumphant, super-spiritual, anointed, pressing-in and overcoming

4. Touch up and embellish your testimony so it sounds far more dramatic and entertaining. Fotoshoppe 10 will also add a few Damascus road moments when the earth shook and there were blinding lights in the sky, passers-by were impressively converted and your feet haven't touched the ground since

5. Add a shiny halo to any recent selfies

6. Conveniently overlook any failures or doubts or misgivings you might have

7. Separate your spiritual and normal life so you can concentrate on making your 'Christian' life shine shine shine

8. Place you in any faith building picture. Scenarios include: walking on water, holding back the tide, closing lions' mouths, preaching to millions, and juggling with poisonous snakes

9. Remove any worry about integrity. No need to be concerned about every day problems such as truth and reality spoiling and discolouring your presentations any more

10. Protect you from well known viruses like honesty, weakness, irony, wrestling and laughing at yourself

So why not get Fotoshoppe 10 today?

Transform every single ordinary moment of the day into a time of excitement and revelation!

Just go to www.AddowbyFaithLift.com.

It's heavenly! And absolutely FREE!!

(Just requires a donation of £199.99)

The Poet In The Rust Bucket

Themes: The God who knows us and is with us in life's difficulties
Bible Refs: Isaiah 43 vv 1-4

He rolled up in an old corroded sports car – a brown rust bucket of a classic. I'm no car man so I'd be guessing at the make and model. Let's just say it was an oxymoron. Clearly a star in its day, but now gone to seed. Drips of brown moisture dropped from the exhaust as it pulled up ahead of me.

'Give you a lift?' he called.

He had a tidy goatee, surfer blond hair and ear studs. I figured it was worth the chance. I'm normally too cautious to go hitching in life, but this wasn't life.

'I'm trying to write this poem,' he said as we pulled away and the wind snagged at his hair. The car picked up speed, but then coughed and lost it again. The whole journey turned out to be like this. Bursts of life ambushed by jolting, throaty groans.

'I'm no poet,' I said.

'Everyone's a poet,' he said. 'They just don't know it.' He changed gear, the car growled and lurched, so he changed back again. 'So,' he went on, 'This poem of mine. It's about battling through the hard days of life. The empty years, the lonely nights, that sort of thing. You want to hear what I got so far? I need a sounding board.'

'Why not?'

'Do not be afraid…'

'I'm not.'

He laughed. 'No pal, this is the poem.'

He hit the accelerator and we speeded up, then the exhaust spat watery smoke and we slowed down again.

'Do not be afraid,' he said, 'for I've ransomed you.

I have called you by name; you're mine.

When you go through deep waters I will be with you.

When you battle through great trouble, I'll be there.

When you travel through rivers of difficulty, you will not drown.

When you walk through the fire of oppression, you will not be burned up.'

Silence, apart from the throaty roar of the engine. The wind blew dust on our faces then gusted it off again.

'What d'you think, pal?' he said eventually.

'It's good. What's it mean?'

'It's about the divine presence. You see I guess that many people expect that when life is good, God is there. I want to tell them, that God is there when life is hard. When it's bitter and twisted. When it threatens to crush and destroy. He's no less present when you and I are cornered and struggling.'

Taken from the biblical novel *Breaking into The Good Book* by Dave Hopwood.

The Quiet

Themes: Jesus praying, and creating the world, and his close relationship with his father

Bible Refs: Mark 1 vv 35-39

For a while he is with his father again and he is free. The years of oppression and restriction fall away. They are in the mountains together, creating wild goats and waterfalls. Running, splashing, constructing, laughing, seeing the world come alive as they talk and sing and create. He is in his element. They leave a trail of rugged landscapes and fierce creatures in their wake, along with tiny flowers and delicate insects...

In the breaking dawn he prays and talks and loses himself in the wonder of it all once again. The world being born. Then a voice breaks in, and another.

People want you, they need you. They've come back looking for you again, he is told. It's his friends, concern written all over their faces, they are on an earnest quest to bring him back to reality. He listens, thinks, sighs, and lifts his face to the heavens. He nods.

'Let's move on,' he says.

'But the people, they're asking for you...'

'I know. But there are others we need to see. Other places to visit. We can't say yes to everyone. We need to keep moving. Let's go.'

He stands and brushes the dirt from his knees. His friends scratch their heads then gather their stuff, more than they needed to bring, and they move on. The creating must continue. Bringing glimpses of resurrection to the lives of the struggling...

Voting

Themes: The death of Jesus and its meaning
Bible Refs: John 3 v 16, Philippians 2 vv 5-8

A couple of angels are chatting in heaven.

1. Why's it so quiet round here? Where's all the usual music and laughter and creative spark?
2. It'll be time to vote soon.
1. Oh right, and I suppose he's worried about which way to vote. Needs some time to consider.
2. Oh no. he decided long ago.
1. Rrrrright… so why the sombre atmosphere?
2. It's a tough decision.
1. But you said he's already made it.
2. Yes. But that makes it no easier.
1. Well, let's hope it makes a difference.
2. Oh it'll make a difference all right.
1. Really? Because there are many times voting seems to do very little good.
2. Well not this time. This will make a difference trust me.
1. Okay. When does he vote? Is it soon?
2. Friday.

1. And where's the polling station?

2. That hill down there.

1. Outside?

2. Yep.

1. That's not very private. Puts a cross in a box does he?

2. No. He puts it on that hill over there.

1. Won't it blow away?

2. It's made of wood.

1. Still. It's not very private though is it?

2. That's the point. He wants everyone to know who he's voting for, so he's putting a cross right up there on a hill. For everyone to see.

1. And who's he voting for?

2. The whole works. People. The planet. The universe. The entire creation gets a Yes.

1. Wow! That's a big vote.

2. And a painful one. It'll cost him everything.

1. And er… will things cheer up round here then?

2. Not right then. Three days after. There'll be a party then.

1. I look forward to that.

2. Everyone's looking forward to that.

They leave.

The Big Day

Themes: The return of Jesus
Bible Refs: Mark 13 vv 32-45

An angel (2) is on the phone. A second one enters (1).

1. Hold the phone, it's off again.

2. What? (He lowers the phone)

1. Cancelled. Well, postponed.

2. You're kidding.

1. Nope.

2. Not again. But this is the 14,573rd time we've had to stop everything. I've got 6 billion flyers printed and ready to go. WITH THE DATE ON!

1. Well, can you use them for something else? Like wallpaper or notepaper, or... or loo paper. Oh no, we don't need loos up here do we...

2. Are you sure about this, I mean there's a bloke in Milton Keynes who's absolutely adamant it was today. And a woman in Texas concurred. It had gone viral. It was all over Facebook and Twitter and YouTube. They were pretty sure down there on that tiny

planet. Spielberg, Lucas and Jackson are topping the box office with a movie version. And One Direction are number one with a song about it.

1. Yes well, they've been pretty sure hundreds of times over the last two thousand years. And look – we're still waiting.

2. What about the catering though? I'd booked 25 million ice cream vans and twice that number of hot dog stands. Plus 27,000 jugglers.

1. Jugglers?

2. Yea, to entertain the crowd as they queue up to meet him. It'll be a long wait surely.

1. Don't think so, it'll happen in the blink of an eye. And every one'll see him at once.

2. Oh, so there's no call for 15 million wide screen cinema screens then, you know to broadcast it live?

1. Nope. And I doubt you'll need those flyers. When it happens – it'll be obvious.

2. What about the warm-up band? I'd booked the heavenly choir to play a few numbers, you know – Here Comes the Son, No More Knocking on Heaven's Door, Heaven Isn't a Place on Earth… that sort of thing.

1. Cancel the lot.

2. When will it be then? Come on, give us a clue, you move in some big circles, you must know?

1. No. I've told you. None of us know. Not here, not on planet earth, not in some far flung corner of the universe. Doesn't matter how much people claim to have seen it in the skies, or read it in the papers, or discovered it in a Christian paperback. Even He doesn't know. And if He doesn't know you can bet your non-existent wings that a man in Milton Keynes doesn't know either.

2. What about a woman in Texas?

1. No! No, no, no. No one knows. Only His Father.

2. (Sighs and nods) Right, well I'll sort it then. AGAIN. I'll have to call and cancel the ambulance people, the stewards, the police AGAIN... all the legal forms will be wasted, they were dated for today. It wasn't like this when he was on earth, you know. No health and safety to worry about when he was feeding 5000 people. Just happened. We didn't do a risk assessment when those four guys ripped up his roof to get their friend healed. We didn't need insurance when he went walking on water...

They exit, looking frustrated.

The Sermon

Themes: God's manifesto
Bible Refs: Luke 4 vv 16-21

We went to church.

We arrived late and there were a lot of people. So it was standing room only. It was a beautiful warm day, perfect for a wedding, and the inside of the little church was cool and full of the smell of flowers. We slipped down a side aisle and hid behind a pillar. I was surprised to see Jack and Jimmy there, and blow me, Si too. Had Josh invited them? Why? Everything was kosher for a while, boring but kosher. Not having a seat proved to be an advantage as we didn't have to bother about all that stand up, sit down, kneel down malarkey. But then the preacher got up and the sermon started. The preacher was the local vicar, been around for years. I didn't know him but my old man had done some furnishing work on his house and they'd been on nodding terms ever since.

The old guy was having a bit of trouble reading the Bible bit before he started talking, the print was too small or his glasses were the wrong sort. That's when Josh stuck a finger in the air and volunteered to read it for him. There was a bit of a commotion at first 'cause this was well unplanned, but then Josh's cousin, the bride, saw it was him and looked well chuffed that he'd volunteered. Josh gave her a big grin and stepped up to read.

'Many have dreamt of freedom. Of captives set free, wrongs put right, cruelty replaced with justice, abuse displaced by kindness. Martin Luther King dreamt. So did Ghandi. Mandela, Mother Teresa and Bono. They all dreamt and the dream goes on and with the living of their lives they give their dream to us. But today I'm here to tell you – this is more than a dream. The dream is giving birth to reality. You see, the God of hope is coming, and actually is already here, heavily disguised. In the cracks, in the shady corners, in the mess and the stains of everyday life. In the slums and the brothels, in the whispers of the humble and the screams of the wounded. He sits in dark prisons and ill-equipped hospitals, in the foodless kitchens and freezing homes. He's the eyes of the blind and ears for the deaf. Life for the dead and freedom for captives. The great Eddie Izzard once described the church as a place full of people with no muscles in their arms. Well, wake up, cause I've come to put the muscles back.'

Taken from *Sons of Thunder* (a modern retelling of the gospel) by Dave Hopwood, pub. Authentic Media.

A Long Time Ago…

Themes: A retelling of the life of Jesus for Star Wars day, (May the 4th be with you)
Bible Refs: Philippians 2 vv 5-11, Romans 5 vv 15-17

A long time ago, in a galaxy far, far away
A time of peace was ticking away.
When an empire of darkness laid siege to the land
And the empire of light knew the end was at hand.

The evil Darth who perpetrated the plot
Rebelled against the good things he'd got.
Once a Jedi Knight, he turned his back on good
And dragged a third of the empire through the mire and the mud.

The benign dictator in the empire of light
Feared for the future of goodness and right
If the evil Darth were to win the day
Then destruction and darkness would soon have their way.

So the benign dictator hatched a cunning plan
He assembled his forces – selected a man.
A Knight of sorts, with a sabre of light,
This was the man he selected to fight.

This Jedi Knight, with truth at his hip
Took to the skies in some kind of ship.
Flew into the fray and confronted the Darth
And they met for the mother of all battles on earth.

Well the battle ensued, lasting three years,
There was war in the heavens and blood, sweat and tears,
Then, just as things turned in the Jedi's favour
The evil Darth floored him with a slice of his sabre.

With a silent scream he struck the Jedi's head
And in a few short hours, the hero was dead.
The dark side had triumphed, to the Jedi's cost.
And with the good knight destroyed the battle was lost.

The evil Darth then assembled his might,
Prepared to invade the empire of light.
Then a rumbling began as low as thunder,
And the shaking that followed tore the dark side asunder.

The forces assembled there panicked and fled
As a Jedi Knight lifted his head.
The evil Darth stared in horror and said,
"This cannot be so, the Jedi was dead."

But the Jedi was back – the story was true,
With a stroke of his sabre he cut the Darth in two.
The evil prince fell writhing away
And the empire of darkness crumbled that day.

The outcome was clear, the dark side lay dying.
But it wouldn't give up, it still went on trying;
And back in the galaxy far, far away
The Jedi battles, even today.

This fable, this story, this plot that you hear
Relates to a planet not too far from here.
In fact, the Jedi Knight once did battle on earth
And his victory bought justice, hope and self-worth.

Fear leads to anger and anger to hate
And hate to death and by then it's too late.
So the benign dictator intervened and stepped in
Sending his son to fight death… and to win.

The Quest

Themes: A parable about Jesus
Bible Refs: John 14 vv 1-6

One day an explorer decided to go on a quest to find God. He wasn't too sure about the whole thing – he thought there might be some form of deity out there somewhere, but didn't know what that meant; and to be honest he was more than a little fearful of what he might find. But he steeled himself and started the search.

He went to the city library and spent a long time studying charts and maps. They offered up no answers, at least nothing he recognised. So he made calls to various teachers and seers, to wise women and men, and visited each one. They offered their various creative and colourful theories as to the whereabouts of any gods, but ultimately the man came away confused. Eventually he sat down on a park bench and sat chewing on his thumb nail. That was when he noticed the figure sitting opposite him. The stranger glanced over and smiled. That was the moment when the explorer realised he'd spotted this figure before, just here and there, passing by as he went on his way.

'Can I be of any help?' the stranger asked.

The man wasn't sure, but something about the figure reassured him.

'Maybe,' he said.

They walked all day. The explorer and the stranger. And the stranger showed the man places he knew well, yet hadn't explored at all. He revisited moments from the explorer's past and showed him things he had missed the first time, he led him to people he knew well, yet didn't know at all. And in every encounter the stranger was careful and compassionate, yet searing and insightful. They laughed together, ate good food, talked, and argued from time to time. And the darkness began to fall.

'I have to go now,' the stranger said quietly and he turned and walked away, leaving the man on the same bench he'd been sitting on when they first met.

The stranger walked away and melted into the darkness. Moving, it seemed, from one dimension to another. And as he went the explorer realised. He had met God and it had not been as expected. He had not been disappointed or fearful. He had been many other things instead. And now it was up to him. He sat thinking for quite a while, reflecting on the day.

The night closed in, and the cold came with it. But he barely noticed. Eventually, and cautiously, he nodded to himself, stood up and walked away from the bench, resolved to become a different kind of explorer.

Jonah's Song

Themes: Jonah and the whale
Bible Refs: Jonah 1-4

I was so deep in thought and so desperate that I didn't notice the hole in the ground till it swallowed me up. I landed at the bottom of some stone steps. Technicolor graffiti lined the stone walls and a guy with creamy dreadlocks and a dirty caftan was strumming a guitar. The tune had a good groove to it and as I got nearer he threw in some words.

I ran for a long time and boarded a boat
I'd get on anything that looked like it could float
I wanted to get away from the call of God
The call to go to Nineveh was dangerous and odd.

His voice was a mix between Bob Dylan and Tracey Chapman, which was unusual to say the least. But the sound was good and he acknowledged me with a nod as I slowed up to listen. I felt obliged then to hang around. I looked for a hat full of coins on the ground but there was nothing.

So I got on this boat and I sailed the other way
Then a storm blew up at the height of the day
I was fast asleep but the crew woke me up
And when they told me about it I knew what was up.

The storm wasn't normal – it was plain divine
I knew I had to put my life on the line
So I told them 'Throw me over and I'll see you round'
And they hurled me in the waves and I fell down, down.

Then the strangest thing, a fish came along
And this is the weirdest part of the song
Many folks claim that I made it up
But I kid you not the fish swallowed me up.

Inside the beast was no game of skittles
So I got on my knees amongst the food and the spittle
And I talked to God and I changed my mind
And I told him my life was right there on the line.

So the whale got sick and he felt real sore
And he threw me up on Nineveh's shore
I walked around preaching and covered in vomit
And those Ninevites sure got the message from it.

They prayed and fasted and laid their lives on
the line
And God took a look and changed his mind
He didn't want to kill them, he wanted them
back
And I felt like I'd been stabbed in the back.

I knew he'd turn around and forgive those folk
After I'd walked round looking like one big joke
Being a prophet ain't the kind of life you'd wish
There are days when I'd rather just be a big fish.

So I found some shade from the heat of the day
And would you know it – the shade withered
away
I was mad with God for letting me fry
And I told him he'd better just let me die.

But he answered me back after not too long
Told me I'd got my priorities wrong
The loss of one plant had filled me with pity
But God cared about all these people in the city.

That's about the end of this really strange tale.
You may know it as Jonah and the whale
It'll be round forever to tell the people all
Not to be surprised when God gives a call.
Not be surprised when God gives a call.
Not to be surprised when God gives a call…

He went back to strumming the tune. I felt in my pockets for a couple of coins and laid a few in a little stack in front of him. He'd shut his eyes now and wasn't watching. I waited to see if he'd spot my generosity but there was nothing from him. So then I wondered about picking up the coins again as he didn't seem bothered, but I heard footsteps coming and realised I couldn't be seen stealing a busker's wage. I moved on quickly, breaking into a run as the words of the song rattled around the backstage of my mind.

Taken from the biblical novel *Breaking Into the Good Book* by Dave Hopwood.

The Garage And The Mayor

Themes: A retelling of the evil farmers parable
Bible Refs: Matthew 21 vv 33-43

There was a town with a very generous mayor. He bought new cars for everyone and for a while everyone was fine. But then the cars began to break down, so the mayor appointed a family to open a garage to fix the cars. He provided the capital for them to buy the property and start the business. But the workers in the garage spent most of their time working on their own cars and ignoring the rest of the town. One or two of the mechanics cared about the other cars and tried to encourage the other mechanics to help the whole town, but all to no avail. Eventually the garage ran out of money and went bust.

So the mayor sent his son along, who was a gifted mechanic, and he travelled around the town and began fixing the broken cars. He did this for three years, but the family at the garage grew resentful, especially when he challenged them about their failure to do their job. So one night they ambushed him, took him away and murdered him.

The town was broken-hearted, because they had lost a friend, a gifted mechanic who cared about putting their cars right. But it wasn't over. One Sunday morning stories began to ripple through the town. Some of the locals were claiming to have seen the mechanic again, alive and well. The family at the garage tried to silence the rumours but the more they tried the more the stories spread. More and more people claimed to have seen the mechanic, and after a while they wrote their stories down. The stories were passed on from generation to generation and these inspired the people to fix cars in the way that the mechanic had done. They often came up against opposition, but showed incredible courage and tenacity in the face of trouble. Word spread and the work went on until a billion lives had been affected.

Body Parts

Themes: We are all different
Bible Refs: 1 Corinthians 12

I don't know if Paul was into cartoons but the picture he sketches in 1 Corinthians 12 about bits of the body could well make a good Pixar short. An ear wanders up to an eye (presumably on its own legs) and mutters about wanting to leave the rest of the body. And then a foot comes hopping along demanding that it be set free from the leg it's on. It's a scene of mumbling and complaining where various parts of the body are disappointed with their lot. Before long, no doubt, the kidney and the liver will go five rounds with each other, and the bottom will be playing rock paper scissors against the funny bone. Add a couple of sisters, a singing snowman and a lot of ice and hey! you've got Frozen 2!

What's it all for? Paul's gone into the realms of Loony Toons in order to make the point that the body of Jesus is a wonderful mish-mash of diverse parts. And we're not all the same, doing the same job. We have different roles to play, drawing on our personalities, experiences, strengths and weaknesses. I take a lot of encouragement from that, as I often feel on the outside looking in, not able to find my place in the ordinary way of Christian things. If there is such a thing. But thank God, we can all find our place, and we don't have to ape what others are doing. If I'm the ear wax in the body then I'm doing a vital job. The body would have problems without me. I may not be the best looking, but I'm there for a reason. Here's a little anecdotal piece on the subject of feeling different.

It's as if they are standing outside a shop window, in fact a whole row of shop windows, a couple of small children with their noses pressed against the glass, peering in. And they are quite happy there, happy on their own, happy to look on. But every so often one of them gets the feeling that he or she should be inside one of the shops, even though experience has shown them they would feel ill at ease in there. So they question themselves and their place outside those windows. There are plenty of others with them, if only they might take the time to notice. And thankfully the landowner is out there too. He's a man who gets about, happy in the shops and happy outside of them, and happy for the boy and girl to be where they are. More than happy, he encourages them to make the most of their place out there. To relax and prosper on that pavement and, when they have the chance, to tell those inside the shops what they see. The most difficult times come when they are invited inside the shops by others, because they know they'll feel total aliens in there. Lonely, even though the place is crowded. They are best outside looking in and passing on what they see. Plunge them into the world of the shops and they are painfully at sea. Often drowning. Fortunately, when that happens, the landowner comes to the rescue, dragging them to safety and the solid ground of the street outside. It's tempting to be complacent on their strip of solid ground, but there's always more to see, more to learn, as they wrestle to accept that they are outside and others are in there. And from time to time they are reminded of the landowner's patience and are grateful for his kindness as he waits with them on that street, and paces those pavements alongside them.

Lost Treasure

Themes: The parable of hidden treasure
Bible Refs: Matthew 13 vv 44-46

And it came to pass that there was a time when everyone believed in themselves and some things had been lost in the chaotic past. They worked and played and rested and made love, laughed and cried, had families and enemies and friends, and fashioned their own forms of reality. Many good things had prevailed. And so had the wars. Sadly people still found reasons to battle with one another, sometimes using words, at other times bombs and bullets. Ideologies came and went and people thought them worth killing and dying for.

And one day a young man, living near one of the battle zones and short of food, came upon an empty scrap of land. He stole a spade and began digging the ground, looking for lost gold or rotting food. He'd fought many battles of his own, believed in the fighting back then. But not anymore. With a broken heart and scars lacing his body his fighting was done. He'd loved and lost too many times.

The sweat was building on his brow and he wasn't having much luck with his digging when the metal of his spade struck something. It wasn't a rock or a bit of bombshell or a body, and didn't have the crunch of anything edible, so he fell on his knees and began scrabbling in the dirt like a dog. Soon his fingers connected with something oblong and smooth. He worked it free. It was a book. An old, mildewed leather-bound book. He smeared away the mud and the damp and flicked it open. Books were rare these days and the feel of the wafer thin pages was strange and mysterious in his fingers. It wasn't a novel or a textbook, but something more.

And as he read he forgot about his hunger and found another appetite developing within him. He couldn't put it down. He'd never come across these kind of things before. Hours tripped by, it grew dark and began to rain. The pages flinched as the heavy drops spattered them. He looked up. Night had fallen. The sound of shelling echoed in the distance. He grabbed the spade and made for his shelter, a shack in the woods a few miles away. He'd get no sleep now. Not tonight. He needed to finish the book, and then he needed to do something about it.

Wilderness Days

Themes: Jesus tempted in the wilderness
Bible Refs: Matthew 4 vv 1-11

It was a body blow, this latest challenge. Bread and stones were one thing (he'd soon be making bread but not this way, feeding thousands from practically nothing), but using this kind of ammunition from Psalm 91. That was fighting dirty. The words were so precious, so powerful. God looks after those he loves. He'll protect them from harm and safety. The angels will catch them when they fall, the stones won't dash them to pieces. A sign of God's compassion. And here they were being twisted, like a scalpel being used to damage rather than heal.

'Throw yourself off here, you can trust God, he'll catch you. If he is your father, if he truly loves you.'

That was the essence of the message. And that hurt. He trusted his God, cared for him, and he trusted those words from Psalm 91. But if he resisted proving them, wasn't it tantamount to disrespect? If he didn't throw himself down for the angels to catch and for God to protect, what then? Was he doubting his father's love and protection? Wasn't the very act of throwing himself off a sign of launching himself into God's arms before he began his three-year mission?

The words swam in his mind like disorientated fish. The phrases bumping against each other. Like missiles meeting across a battlefield and cancelling each other out. Little explosions rocking his world and shattering his confidence. He glanced down and for a moment he saw himself falling, and those angels, those guardians he knew so well, swooping in for a dramatic rescue. A statement of faith. He braced himself for the leap. Leant backward and pushed off. As he dived into the unknown those words repeated in his mind like a song with the kind of hook that stays with you all day. For he orders his angels to protect you wherever you go. They will hold you with their hands to keep you from striking your foot on a stone. The LORD says, 'I will rescue those who love me.'

His father loves him and this rescue will show it. He fell.

And then he opened his eyes. Looked down. His feet were still on the edge, on the very edge of the highest point of the temple complex, stones crumbling and falling away as his weight pressed on them. There was no need to jump. He would launch himself soon enough, and his father would be with him. But not like this. For a moment a shadow crossed his mind, would there be a time when his father would turn away? What if there was a day when the message of this psalm was upended, and his father would hold back for the sake of love? A day when he might be rejected, abandoned, totally alone, for the very purpose of his father's love for others? The angels staying back, nothing to stop him being dashed on the rocks, for the sake of the planet, for the sake of other lives, for the sake of the cosmos. If so this decision, here today, this would only serve to strengthen his resolve. He wouldn't test that love. He would trust it. A sudden fleeting glimpse exploded in his mind's eye – the broken, the lost, the prisoners of darkness, a world falling apart and misused. He flinched at the sudden sound of a distant nail being hammered, not a carpentry nail, another kind. He shuddered and kicked at a nearby stone and pondered this. Then, whispering words from Deuteronomy, he stepped back from the edge and turned away.

The Good Samaritan – Take 2

Themes: The Good Samaritan
Bible Refs: Luke 10 vv 25-37

(Enter two people in conversation about an event they are planning)

1. Right, let's get down to planning this event. I thought the reading about the parable of the Good Samaritan from the gospel of Luke would be a good one as the theme is Caring for Others.

2. Sounds okay, remind me of the story again.

1. Well, this guy is travelling along a road when he gets attacked and beaten by a gang of thugs.

2. Oh no, we can't have that.

1.Why not?

2. There could be children or people of a nervous disposition present. That's too 15 rated. We need it more PG.

1. More PG?

2. Yes! PG! Parental Guidance. We can't have Jesus telling violent stories – he's not Quentin Tarantino!

1. Haven't you heard the one about the wedding guests who got slaughtered for not coming to the party?

2. No!

1. Well the shocking nature of the story is just Jesus's way of telling us this stuff is serious and it matters.

2. Fair enough, but let's concentrate on this one. We'll have to change it a bit. Let's er… massage it a little. Say the man was…

1. What? Surrounded by a bunch of five year olds who stuck their tongues out at him?

2. Don't be ridiculous! No, let's say the man fell. Tripped, fell, knocked his head, and was lying there feeling a bit woozy.

1. Woozy? There was most likely blood. He looked half dead.

2. Oh we can't have blood. It's not an episode of Casualty. Yes, the man fell over and was a bit woozy.

1. But the reason a priest didn't stop to help him was because he was worried about making himself ritually unclean. If the man was actually dead or dying he couldn't have contact with him. The man sitting there looking a bit dazed wouldn't have been a

problem for the priest. He could easily have given the man a hand up.

2. Let's just say the priest had a headache. He was feeling a bit…

1. What – woozy?

2. No! He was on a bad day and had a bit of man-flu. Didn't see the man and went past him. In fact he didn't want to give him his cold.

1. And what about the next guy? The Levite – the assistant to the priest.

2. He er… he had… hayfever. He was feeling all heady and er…

1. A bit woozy?

2. No, stop it with the woozy. No one's feeling woozy.

1. I thought you said the guy who'd been beaten up was feeling woozy.

2. Oh yes he was! But he hadn't been beaten up, he just tripped over something…

1. What – like the inconsistencies in this story?

2. No. He tripped over and was slumped by the road. But there was no blood or bruises or vomit or anything distasteful.

1. Ah but what about the Samaritan? The man who helped him.

2. What about him?

1. He was distasteful. They would have all hated him – all the characters – the man who slipped on the banana skin, the priest with the lurgy, and his assistant with the hangover…

2. Hayfever!

1. Oh yea, hayfever. They all hated Samaritans.

2. No one is hating anyone. They're all good friends. Samaritans are nice, more than nice. They help millions of people every year.

1. Yes, now they do. But that's because of this story. Back then Samaritans were sworn enemies of the Jews. That's why this story's countercultural. It's about reaching across boundaries and breaking taboos.

2. We don't need to mention taboos. A man trips up, two people go past who aren't feeling too well, and then a nice kind Samaritan comes along and takes him somewhere…

1. To an inn. A pub.

2. No. Too much alcohol. To a Travel Inn. Or a Little Chef. And they all live happily ever after.

1. Apart from the Samaritan who might well have been beaten up by a gang of locals when he came out of the er… Little Chef. Wonder if

there was anyone passing by to help him? Or maybe everybody had a hangover.

2. Hayfever! And you're just complicating the story. Jesus kept it nice and simple.

1. Yea. And full of violence and muggers and bad guys and taboos.

2. Be quiet. Just go away, clean it up and make it acceptable.

1. I think I need to lie down, I'm feeling a bit woozy…

They walk off.

The Inedibles

Themes: Noah and the ark
Bible Refs: Genesis 7 vv 1-5

The sheep and cows and doves are strutting their stuff. They've got lots of friends. They feel very confident indeed. The locusts feel good too. Fourteen of every kind of chopping, cutting, hopping, dissecting, snipping-in-two, nibbling, chewing and spitting-out locusts. Lots of them. Whole gangs. They're happy. They're in the majority, this is locustville right now. Whereas the pigs and the lizards and the bats. They look well worried. An argument breaks out.

'Why's there only two of us and fourteen of you?' say the pigs.

'Get over it,' sneer the cows, 'you're just not that important.'

Noah appears.

'Right you lot you're probably wondering why there are only two of some of you. Yet fourteen of others.'

'No... No, no, no, no. Never crossed our minds. Not at all.'

'Well, I have good news and I have bad news. Oh and then even worse news. Which would you like first – the bad, good or very bad?'

They decide to start with the bad – somewhere in the middle of the scale.

'Well I've been chatting with the almighty, you know, the one who created all of you lot… and well, I think we'd all agree he was pretty clever wasn't he? I mean, how many different kinds of locusts would you have thought of? Yes, that's true, I'm not sure that we really need so many different kinds of locusts… but… yes and I've never understood the purpose of wasps. But that's not the point. The point is – it's gonna rain. For a long time. What's rain? Well, water is gonna drop out of the sky on your heads. Yes, now would be a good time for God to invent the umbrella, I agree. But he's not. Instead he's invented me, and I've invented a boat. What? That big thing behind me. Yes… it will float. It will. IT WILL! And the good news is – you've all won free tickets. So you get to go on the boat, sail off into the sunset and then wait for the water to… er… go off somewhere. I dunno where… never seen so much water before so I don't know what happens to it. Maybe it'll all turn into mashed potato and you can eat it all. Anyway after that you'll all get off…. apart from the ones who won't get off. Which brings me to the really bad news. Now any questions? Eh? What is the really bad news? Ah, now I'm glad you asked that, it's not easy for me to say, put it like this, those of you in the larger groups, yep that's right the ones singing and dancing and feeling good about yourselves 'cause there's a lot more of you, well there won't always be a lot more of you. What am I saying? Well, don't go making too many career plans… or putting a deposit on a holiday. I mean, you'll all be coming off the boat, it's just that some of you will be coming off inside some of the others.

(Sighs) 'All right, what I'm trying to say is… I'm allowed to bring fourteen of every kind of creature that we can… ahem… eat. Right, shall we get on board? Look there's no need to panic, we may not have to eat all of you. We don't know how long we'll be on the boat. If we're only on for a few hours then a snack will suffice. A few locusts and half a sheep will be fine. Well you can draw straws. On the other hand if we're there for a few weeks then… Where you all going? You can't leave. You've won the special tickets. You're coming on board. You're the lucky ones. It's a great opportunity. Something to tell the grandchildren. Except of course, for those for whom it'll be less of an opportunity and… there won't be any grandchildren. What? I dunno. Fried? Steamed? Sautéed? In a white wine sauce? What would you prefer? Steamed is obviously healthier. Well not for you, no. I was thinking of me. Anyway look, there's no time to waste. Can't stand here prattling all day about consuming you lot. All aboard. Edibles on the left, inedibles on the right.'

Taken from *Pulp Gospel* by Dave Hopwood.

The Biggest Risk

Themes: Jesus's mission
Bible Refs: Philippians 2 vv 4-8

Two heavenly bureaucrats walk on. 2 has a handful of papers.

1. So let's get down to business.

2. Well there's just one item on the agenda really – this proposal of a trip to earth.

1. Right. What's the story there?

2. Well – it's about a trip – that's being proposed – to earth.

1. Yes I think I got that the first time. How many involved?

2. Just the one.

1. Just the one! (Sharp intake of breath) We'll have to do a serious bit of risk assessment on that. Who are we talking about?

(2 shows 1 a piece of paper)

1. Oh! Right. Well… I guess if he were to go with a full cohort of angelic warriors in reserve he should be fine.

2. No, he doesn't want that. He wants to go alone.

1. Alone? Well, all right. It's possible – if he takes an invisibility cloak and a light sabre.

2. Nope. None of those either.

1. Really? How long does he want to go for? I guess an hour might be okay.

2. Longer.

1. (Another intake of breath) Okay, half a day could be doable, if he keeps his head down.

2. How about thirty-three years?

1. Thirty-three years!

2. Thirty-three years.

1. Hmm. Only if we can send him somewhere safe, peaceful, tranquil. Say New Zealand. Or Oxford.

2. Can't send him to Oxford – have you never seen Lewis – three murders a week.

1. How about a little Yorkshire village?

2. How about Israel?

1. Israel? Without backup and a light sabre? With everything that's going on there? You're kidding!

2. Nope. That's the plan. Thirty-three years in Roman occupied Israel, climaxing with a trip to Jerusalem at Passover.

1. Oh perfect. The place'll be full of soldiers and revolutionaries, all armed to the teeth. He won't last three days. (He sighs) All right, enough talking, I think we'd better get this down in black and white. So you have a risk assessment form there? Thanks. Right. (reading) Point one – Description of Hazard.

2. Son of God entering occupied country. Occupying force famous for violence and murder. Oh and very straight roads.

1. Right. (reading) Full Name of Person in Danger.

2. Yeshua ben Yehosef – Jesus son of Joseph.

1. Doesn't sound very grand, couldn't we do him a t-shirt with Messiah embossed on it. And maybe some wristbands for his friends. WWYBYD. You know – What would Yeshua ben Yehosef do?

2. No – it's a covert operation. And wristbands will never catch on.

1. Fair enough. And I guess he'd better not go telling any of his stories. Those parables of his are enigmatic – they could be seen as offensive and antagonist. Especially towards the religious community.

2. Communal meals?

1. Oh no – he'd better eat alone, or with one or two close friends at most. For one thing we can't protect him in a public place, and secondly you know what he's like. He'll be breaking bread with all the wrong people – criminals, prostitutes, collaborators. Food could be a minefield.

2. Miracles?

1. Keep them to a minimum and strictly on the quiet. Otherwise the crowds'll come running. All he need do is cure someone with a limp and everyone with a touch of man-flu will be desperate for a piece of him. And there's no way we can cover our backs there. People get all kinds of crazy ideas when you get them all together. Whatever you do don't let him feed a crowd – he won't wear sterile gloves when he hands it out, and there'll be no special diets on offer.

1. All right. Next – (reading) Potential Harm.

2. Oh not much. Just verbal abuse, beatings with fists and rods, 39 lashes with a lead-tipped whip, and protracted execution on a Roman cross.

1. There isn't enough space to write all that. Shall I just put Death?

2. I suppose so.

1. (reading) Existing Systems of Safe Controls. What do we have in place to protect him?

2. All kinds of things. Divine power, thousands of angels, burning swords, a skipload of fire from heaven… but he doesn't want any of them. Won't touch them with a celestial barge pole. Says he wants to be more vulnerable. More human.

1. That's just asking for trouble.

2. You're telling me.

1. (reading) Suggested Safe Systems Required. Hmm. Can you tell me – are any others likely to be affected if there's an incident?

2. Yes.

1. Ah good, that'll strengthen our case. Give me some names.

2. That'll be difficult. If there wasn't enough space to describe the potential harm then you've got no hope with this one.

1. Why? How many are we talking about?

2. Three hundred million. And that's just at the moment. Give it a couple of thousand years and we'll be looking at 7 billion. I doubt you'll get all the names in that little box there.

1. Oh this is ridiculous. (reading) Recommendations. (writes) Highly unsafe. Won't pass any of the health and safety

regulations. Recommend calling the whole thing off. Immediately.

2. Right. Brilliant. Excellent idea. Just one snag. You're too late, he's already gone.

1. Too late?

2. Yes, he said he knew this would happen, so he left early. (looks at watch) Should be pitching up in Bethlehem in a few months from now.

1 shakes his head and rips up the paper he is holding. They both walk off.

God Seeks Help

Themes: The existence of God
Bible Refs: Genesis 1 v 1, 1 John 1 vv 1-5

Doctor. So what can I do for you?

God.   I feel depressed.

Doc.   How can you? You're the alpha and omega, the beginning and the end. The almighty, the maker of heaven and earth, you ride on the wings of the morning, you make a chariot of the thunder and lightning, you're the best thing since... well, sliced bread... and hey – you invented all the ingredients for that...

God.   Yea but... I think I'm losing faith in myself.

Doc.   Hmm, well you wouldn't be alone there.

God.   Exactly! I just don't believe in myself anymore. Everyone else has given up on me so I thought I'd join them.

Doc.   Well not exactly everyone.

God.   All right, everyone apart from a few folks who watch Songs of Praise.

Doc.   Yes – and then there's the small matter of the two billion others around the globe.

God.   Really? Two billion? You're kidding?

Doc.   Nope. That's a quarter of the planet.

God.   But I'm so old fashioned, out of date. People have their media-friendly experts and their glossy documentaries about life without me.

Doc.   Are you feeling just a tad threatened?

God.   Yes! It's so frustrating! I just wish they'd come clean and admit that it all comes down to faith. That's why I invented things like vision and imagination, so they could place it in the unseen world. Instead they want to use it to dismiss the mysterious. And they get so angry with me. Especially when bad things happen. It's not my fault you know.

Doc.   They seem to think it is.

God.   'Course they do. Who causes global warming? God. Who makes people drive like lunatics and injure people? God! Who makes people greedy? Oh that'll be God. Why did I stub my toe? Yep – God again. No one wants responsibility anymore.

Doc.   Maybe you need a holiday.

God.   I tried that. But it's impossible. Everybody else works on Sunday these days, they keep me so busy. Oh it's so unfair you know. Coincidence, that's what they call it. I'm running around like a cheetah on Prozac making lots of useful things happen and they call it coincidence. What's a creator to do?

Doc. You never used to be like this. Are you burning out?

God. No, but the planet is. Oh… maybe I should just retire.

Doc. Yes you could let your son take over.

God. Too late, too many other people have already taken over. It was never supposed to be like this. I tried everything. Freedom of choice, guidelines, wise spokespeople, leaders, what's left?

Doc. What about going down to see them? Show them what matters?

God. We talked about that. It's possible. But it's so violent down there at times. Anything could happen.

Doc. Not to you. You're God! Just go down there in a bulletproof suit with a few million henchmen and float about doing some good. What's not to like?

God. Hmm. I thought about that. But it has to be the other way. They don't need another powerbroker down there. They need someone else. Someone… weaker. Someone they can relate to. A different kind of leader.

Doc. Really? That's a risk.

God. Tell me about it. And for them as much as me. If I make myself smaller I'll be looking for their help. It wouldn't be the God of zzzapping and thunder and big smoky mountains anymore, more like a partnership, them and me going into business together. It's a big risk, I've seen how some of them operate.

Doc. Sounds weird to me. Will you do it?

God. Hmmm… got to do something. Watch this space. How much do I owe you for this session?

Doc. (Glances at clock. Sighs.) Nothing – as usual. You never use up any time.

God. Ah yes, time. Can't be doing with it, not where I come from. See you next week.

Doc. A lot can happen in seven days.

God. Yea, like a whole universe… see you.

Dark Morning

Themes: The resurrection of Jesus
Bible Refs: John 20 vv 1-18

She wakes.

Her eyes are dead.

Seen too much murder disguised as punishment.

She stands, washes, tries to convince herself it is worth getting up today. She spots the bundle by the door. Scoops it up, feels the weight and that shiver down her spine. Leaves the house and joins the shadows outside. Just another shadow moving amongst those etchings of moonlight.

With every step her feet make a thud in the dirt. She's always been heavy-footed, but this morning her walking sounds like a series of hammer blows. Thud. Another shiver down the spine.

She had a dream once, it flashed through her mind when she felt a hand lift her out of the dirt. As she heard stones dropping her life raced before her eyes. It was a full life, a future suddenly bright. Hope transmitted in a stranger's smile.

Now the dream lies in bits, like broken furniture in a room of arguments and bad memories.

Thud. More steps. More shivers. She sees another shadow, fears the worst.

But then the figure nods and the woman whispers. They walk on together, she's more aware than ever that her steps scuff and pound the earth. The other woman is so light on her feet, barely makes a sound. Another shadow appears, and another. Soon there is a group of silent witnesses. Any other trip and they'd have been verbally elbowing each other out of the way to make conversation.

But not here, not now.

There's been little sleep amongst them, barely four hours between them. Their eyes all carry death in them. Preparing themselves for the sight they must confront. She presses the bundle closer to her body. One or two of the others have similar bundles.

The garden.

They stop, catch sight of the place in the moonlight. The ground shudders. She thinks at first it's lack of sleep. But the others clearly feel it too. There's a door stone lying loose and skewed, and a cave mouth yawning like an open dragon's den.

Soldiers huddle nearby, they grunt and mutter. But they make no move towards the women.

The women shuffle forward and look inside the dragon's mouth.

There is no monster. But then... there is nothing at all. When they look outside they see the soldiers lying like corpses, faces pushed into the ground. Then the light hits them.

A figure, dazzling as if lit by a thousand torches, sits astride the loose door stone. He speaks and his voice has the sound of a rushing river. Like a hundred shining figures. Phrases like 'been raised' 'was crucified' 'don't be afraid' 'not here' hang in the air like wisps of mist.

The figure urges them into the cave. They look, but don't see, not yet. They turn and run, all their feet pounding heavily now, their bundles left behind, and the spark of life beginning to force the look of death from their eyes.

The Last Brownie

Themes: The flawed nature of the biblical heroes
Bible Refs: 2 Corinthians 4 v 4-10

Cast: Paul, Samson, Gideon, Esther, Ruth, Michal.

Props: Fan mail, plate of brownies

A dinner party. They are passing round a plate of brownies, each taking one as they talk until there is just one left on the plate.

Gideon: Well that was a wonderful meal, Ruth.

Samson: Yes, just like the good old days in Canaan.

Esther: Shall we read the mail?

Michal: Good idea! Let me open one. Oh this one's to Elijah. What a fantastic prophet you were – I'm currently developing my prophetic gifts and am using you as my perfect role model. Yours sincerely – guess who.

Ruth: This one's to Moses. Dear Moses, What an incredible leader you were. Every single day I'm inspired by your leadership skills and impressive handling of the Israelite people. Yours faithfully, David Cameron.

Esther: Here's one for David. It says, Love your work, those lyrics are fantastic, so honest, so meaningful, something for every occasion. Keep writing the psalms. Yours creatively, Andrew Lloyd Webber.

Samson: Dear Paul, you must be such a kind, caring, loving person, the way you write about relationships is fantastic. Yours affectionately, Beyoncé.

Ruth: You know, reading all this fan mail to the big heroes establishes what I've long since suspected, we really are the most desperate lot of underachievers.

Samson: Unfair!

Esther: No, no, I think Ruth's right. In fact, I think we should give the last brownie to the saddest act here.

Michal: Well that's obviously me isn't it?

Ruth: Not necessarily, Michal.

Michal: Oh yes it is. Married to the finest king of all time. He was brave, good-looking. A poet, a musician, a man in uniform, what more could I want. And I threw it all away. Admittedly he walked out on me not long after we got married and then chose to come swanning back into my life years later and just expected me to take up where we left off. And my parents basically forced me into the marriage anyway. I had no choice… I just ended up sad and lonely. So you see it has to be me.

Esther: Well, what about Gideon here. The smallest person, in the smallest family in the smallest clan, in the weakest tribe. That's pretty sad.

Gideon: Yes – and when my big break came what did I do? Went off and hid and made home-made wine. And it tasted terrible.

Ruth: Yes but you did overthrow the Midianites, that's more than I ever did.

Samson: Yes Ruth, what exactly did you do?

Ruth: Exactly. It has to be me. I just got married, lost everyone, worked in a field and got married again. Hardly changed the world. I was just another working mother.

Esther: Yes, but you did come up with a memorable quote about my people will be your people and all that.

Michal: Yes. And your grandson certainly did change the world. Not to mention your great, great, great... whatever grandson. So you're out. Whereas you could have ended up with Samson in your family. Now here's a problem child if ever I saw one. Stubborn, wilful, ignorant, petulant and spoilt.

Samson: I am not! That's not fair.

Michal: And he always wants his own way.

Samson: Don't! But I'll have that brownie.

Esther: Samson – you've worked hard for it. Here.

Paul: Well, wait! What about me?

Samson: Sorry, you think you deserve the last brownie, Paul?

Paul: Well, a shot at it at least.

Samson: You'll have to prove it – this is a good brownie and I have a huge appetite, I'll fight you for it.

Paul: Well... I've felt isolated most of my life, often alone, rejected by the church. Don't feel I fit in really. I've hurt my friends at times, pushed them away. Been misunderstood and misquoted down through the ages. Put every last ounce of energy into what I believe and still didn't see the results. The people I converted went astray; the disciples I nurtured left me. I'm often called big-headed, dominant, dogmatic, sexist, and I've had my failings and mistakes paraded before the world for centuries. And to crown it all I never did get rid of that thorn. It's not easy being me… I wanted to give up many times. Many times.

(Pause. They all look at him then one another. Eventually Esther smiles, and the others laugh)

Esther: Sorry Paul, good try, but that won't get you the brownie…

(She stares at the brownie for a moment)

Esther: However… you have given me an idea. Perhaps what we should really do… is this…

She cuts the brownie into pieces and shares them around so that each person gets one.

Crooks Anonymous

Themes: Moses kills an Egyptian and flees
Bible Refs: Exodus 2

Cast: Connie, Dave, Holly, Suzie, Brian, Hannibal, Moses, Chairperson

Con. Hello, my name's Connie the Crowbar and I can break into anything.

Dave. Hello, my name's Dynamite Dave and I'm a safecracker.

Holl. Hello, my name's Holly the Hacker and I've stolen money from every single one of your bank accounts.

Chair. Well, welcome everyone to Crook's Anonymous – as you can see we invite all our participants to introduce themselves honestly before we begin each meeting. Suzy, would you like to carry on?

Suz: Hello, I'm Suzie Stiletto and I've stabbed most things.

Brian. Hello, I'm Brian the Basher and I've headbutted most things.

Han. Hello, I'm Hannibal the Cannibal and I've eaten most things.

Mos. Hello, I'm Moses – Moses the Murderer.

Chair. Moses, it's your first week – would you like to enlarge on that.

Mos. Not really.

Chair. Yes but perhaps it would be good if you did.

Mos: But it might soil my reputation…

Chair. Moses we have to be honest here. It's level ground – you can say anything – we won't mind.

Mos. Well… it all began when I was born – no before I was born… They passed a law which made babies illegal. So when I popped out my mum had to try and hide me – so she put me in the river…

Chair. Oh dear!

Mos. Oh well, I was in a basket. And there weren't too many crocodiles… or vultures. Anyway – it wasn't the best of starts but I got adopted by the royal family, so that made it a bit better. Then years later I went for a walk, saw a soldier and killed him. As you do.

Chair. Oh! Did you know this soldier?

Mos. No – never seen him before. Just whacked him over the head with a shovel and then buried him… with the same shovel. There was a good reason.

Chair. Of course – he would have started smelling if you hadn't buried him quick.

Mos. No I mean there was good reason for killing him.

Suz. There always is.

Hol. There was a good reason for hacking into all your bank accounts.

Brian. Yea and there was a good reason for headbutting all those people.

Mos. No! I did it to save my people.

Han. Oh that's a good one! Why didn't I think of that one?

Mos. Listen! My people were all being persecuted. They were being beaten…

Dave. Probably by Brian the Basher here…

Mos. No! By the Egyptian Regime. Life was hard and the government was very cruel. So I did what I could to save them.

Chair. What was that?

Mos. I hit a soldier and ran away.

Con. That must have really made them feel better.

Chair. Moses, were you caught?

Mos. No. Well, and yes.

Chair. No and yes?

Mos. The Egyptians didn't catch me…

Con. That's a relief…

Mos. But God did.

Suz. Ooh! That's not a relief.

Mos. No, he made me go back…

Chair. And apologise?

Mos   No actually, he made me go back and do the job properly. It was very hard.

Chair. So you were never caught for your crime?

Mos. No, but there were days when I wish I had been.

Chair. Well, it would be great to hear more of your story sometime Moses, but in the meantime – let me award you your Crooks Anonymous honesty badge. (Pins it on and pats it.) There we go, Moses the Murderer. You've earnt that…

Peter's Bible Reading

Themes: Examples of Peter's mistakes to show that Jesus calls us in spite of our flaws
Bible Refs: Luke 5 vv 1-10, Matthew 14 vv 22-32, Mark 8 vv 27-33, Luke 22 vv 54-62

Intro: Today's Bible reading is brought to you by our special guest – the apostle Simon Peter, who will read extracts from his successful life.

Simon Peter (walking on confidently and beginning to read from a Bible he carries):

One day as Jesus was preaching on the shore of the Sea of Galilee, he noticed two empty boats at the water's edge. Stepping into one of the boats, Jesus asked Simon Peter, its owner, to push it out into the water. Then Jesus sat in the boat and taught the crowds from there. When he had finished speaking, he said to Simon, 'Now go out where it is deeper and let down your nets, and you will catch many fish.' 'Master,' Simon Peter replied, 'we worked hard all last night and didn't catch a thing. But if you say so, we'll try again.' And this time their nets were so full they began to tear! A shout for help brought their partners in the other boat, and soon both boats were filled with fish and on the verge of sinking. When Peter realised what had happened, he fell to his knees before Jesus and cried, 'Oh, Lord, please leave me—I'm not a… good person, I'm… oh dear… too much of an awful, terrible sinner to…'

Ahem… actually you don't want to hear about that. Let me try another reading. (Flips pages of Bible)

Ah yes! This is better. *Jesus Walks on Water*. This is an exciting one.

Afterwards Jesus went up into the hills by himself to pray. Night fell while he was there alone. Meanwhile, the disciples were in trouble on their boat far away from land, for a strong wind had risen, and they were fighting heavy waves. About three o'clock in the morning Jesus came to them, walking on the water. When the disciples saw him, they screamed in terror, thinking he was a ghost. But Jesus spoke to them at once. 'It's all right,' he said. 'I am here! Don't be afraid.' Then Peter called to him, 'Lord, if it's really you, tell me to come to you by walking on water.' 'All right, come on then,' Jesus said. So Peter went over the side of the boat and walked on the water towards Jesus. He was walking steadily on the surface of the water, but then he looked around at the high waves, and he was… absolutely terrified? He began to sink. And he screamed out, 'Help! Help! Save me! Save me…'

Oh dear. Actually I don't think you want to hear that one either. It's not really very interesting.

(Flips pages of Bible) Ah here we are. This is a really good one.

Then Jesus asked them, 'Who do you say I am?' Simon Peter answered, (big smile at the audience) 'You are the Messiah, the Son of the living God.' Jesus replied, 'You are blessed, Simon son of John and I say to you that you are Peter, and upon this rock I will build my church, and I will give you the keys of the Kingdom of Heaven.' Then Jesus began to tell his disciples plainly that he had to go to Jerusalem, and he told them he would be killed, and he would be raised on the third day. But Peter took him aside and corrected him. 'Heaven forbid, Lord,' he said. 'This will never happen to you!'

Jesus turned to Peter and said, 'Get away from... me, Satan! You are a... dangerous trap to me. You are seeing things merely from a human point of view, and not from...' D'you know I'm sure there's a good one here somewhere. (Flips pages of Bible) Err....

(Reads again) The guards lit a fire in the courtyard and sat around it, and Peter joined them there. A servant girl noticed him in the firelight and began staring at him. Finally she said, 'This man was one of Jesus's followers!'

Peter stood up and boldly proclaimed, 'I don't... even... know... the man...' (Pause)

Oh dear. Here ends today's lesson.

Peter walks off sadly.

Paul And The Coats

Themes: The stoning of Stephen
Bible Refs: Acts 7 vv 54-60

Cast: Paul & five others, 1-5   Props: Coats
An anonymous figure (Paul) stands holding a pile of clothes. He watches offstage. There is the sound of a loud raucous shout of "Yes!"
A group of five people come in talking excitedly. One by one they take their coats from him.

Paul. I used to have one like that.

4   Yea, I know.

P.   Sent it to the charity shop.

4.   I know. This is it.

P.   That's not a bad one.

2.   Got it just down the road.

P.   Not from Maximus Man. I bet you paid over the odds for it.

1.   That one's mine.

P.   You're welcome to it. Your wife buy that for you did she?

3.   Does my bum look big in this?

All.   Er…

3.   Don't look!

P.   Whose is this one? Not yours!

5.   Yes, why? Doesn't it suit me?

P.   I don't know.

5.   What d'you think? Does it clash?

1.   Haven't a clue. I'm a man.

5.   You sound as if you don't care!

1.   I don't.

P.   This needs a wash.

2.   It doesn't, I washed it only six months ago.

1.   Well, that's a good job done anyway. (looks offstage)

P.   You can say that again.

2.   He had a lot of stamina didn't he?

3.   Yea, I thought he'd never stop moving.

4.   I kept missing him.

5.   We noticed!

P.   What about the body? What shall we do with it now?

1.   Leave it here. Someone'll clear it away eventually.

2.   Thanks for holding the coats.

3.   You off later?

P.   Yea, I'm off up to Damascus to round up a few more like that loser. (nods offstage)

4.   What was his name again?

5.   Can't remember? Stephen was it?

P.   Doesn't matter now anyway.

1.   Take it easy Saul, we'll see you later. Watch yourself on that Damascus road, the sun's a bit bright you know, it can be blinding. Go careful.

P.   Thanks. But I can take care of myself.

(They pat him on the shoulder, and all leave)

Rahab Gets It Right

Themes: Rahab and the spies
Bible Refs: Joshua 2

Rahab stands ironing clothes.

Rahab:
It's easy to judge people, isn't it? Look at them and make your mind up double-quick... I didn't plan it this way, don't know anyone who did, y'know. Wasn't what I imagined growing up. But don't pity me - don't even think about it. And try hard not to judge. Because it's not as if I've never done anything of value, anything important. I'm even mentioned in the Bible. I'm up there with the superstars... you know, Moses, Abraham - those sort of guys. Yeah, me - "Rahab the Harlot" it says. Oh, I don't mind the description. It's better than some things I've been called.

What happened was this: some men came to my house one night, y'know. Like any other night really, but these men were different. They were from out of town, which wasn't that unusual either, I guess, I get a lot of "visitors ". But I'd heard about these men, or at least heard about their nation. They were Jews, and everyone in

Jericho had heard about them - how their God had done some pretty amazing things for them, like setting them free from Egypt and defeating some powerful kingdoms across the Jordan from us. A lot of folks were dead scared of them. But... well, they were really nice to me. No, not in that way... but, I don't know, it did seem as if they cared about me as a person, y'know?

Anyhow, like I say, it just seemed the right thing to help them out, they were on the run and desperate and asked me to hide them. So I did, on my roof, under some piles of flax, pretty clever, eh? It almost got me into deep trouble. I had to do some, OK, call it lying, to get rid of the king's men when they came looking, but... what can I say, I did it. Me! Too me a lot of courage too. But I reckon it was the right thing to do.

(pause as she thinks for a moment)

It saved my life, my family's too. Those men, they promised they'd spare us when they finally took the town, and they were good to their word. We lived, whereas my neighbours, my friends, my "customers"... they didn't.
No, I'm not proud of everything I've done, show me someone who is. But sometimes... sometimes even I get it right.

The Forgotten Four

Themes: The pain and struggles of various Bible characters

Bible Refs: 2 Samuel 21 vv 8-10, Psalm 88, Job 1 & 2, John 20 vv 24-28

Rizpah (R), Heman (H), Job (J) & Tom (T)

R. Hi Heman – you here again?

H. Yup.

R. Third time this month isn't it?

H. Yup.

R. Me too. Same old same old.

H. It's unfair, Rizpah. You never catch St Paul in here.

(Job walks in)

R. Tell me about it. Wish *I'd* written to the Corinthians. All right there, Job. You back again? In Room 101 with the other forgettables.

J. Obviously. What are you two in for?

H: Same old. No one bothers to read my psalm or write worship songs about Psalm 88, too gloomy. Instead it's all David David David. Psalm 23 and all that. Just the positive bits mind you. He wrote plenty of gloom as well. But no one sings about that anymore. No one thinks a bit of healthy Victor Meldrewing can possibly be included in worship. So I'm consigned to this place. Forgotten. Just because I was honest and wrote my number on a day when I was feeling pretty down in the dumps 'cause my neighbour had kept me up all night, my recycling had been left behind again and I had a cataclysmic headache. I like to think I wrote my psalm for all those folks in the congregation who'd rather strangle the person next to them instead of giving them a cheery hug.

J. Absolutely. I poured my soul into my book. 42 chapters I wrote, and just 'cause they're not full of wonder and miracles everyone avoids them. I'm considering re-doing it as Job-lite. Ten smiley chapters with a few bits of misery tucked away between the shiny, happy 'isn't life a blast' moments. People might find it more palatable then.

R. No! Don't sell out! I know it seems as if people want quick and easy answers, but life isn't like that. They need our songs and stories. Most people are struggling along. When I was on that hillside, grieving over my boys and beating the vultures away, I hung onto the songs of struggling and sadness. People need that, not just happiness and hope. They need reality. It sets them free to be honest.

J. Wow! You've thought this through, haven't you?

R. Every day. Every single day.

(They fall silent for a moment)

H. I do quite like some of David's happy clappy numbers though. Bit of rock'n'roll, you know.

J. Yea, they kept me limping along when the boils were particularly bad.

R' Sure. But our stories complete the picture. Faith doesn't make everything rosy. God's right there in the darkness too. Perhaps especially so. Jesus didn't save the world when he made 180 gallons of free wine. He did it on a tortured hillside.

J. (Sighs) Look at us, eh – the forgotten three. Oh no – the forgotten four, here's another overlooked soul.

(A fourth person, Tom, walks in)

R. Hi, you back again?

T. Yea, I'm fed up. No one sees me as three dimensional, I'm just a walk-on part with weak faith. I was only being honest. Speaking my mind. And what do I get? How do I go down in history? Doubting Thomas. Great. Thanks very much.

R. Come and join us, Tom.

J. Yea, and you know what, 'cause this is a Christian sketch the audience will be expecting a nice neat ending that makes a point.

R. Yes, well, instead, let's just leave it open-ended...

H. So they can make up their own minds.

T. Ooh... I doubt if they'll like that...

(All walk off)

Human Haiku

A Haiku – a poem in 3 lines and 17 syllables
(5,7,5)

True humanity
Is a very godly thing.
Kindness, hope, courage.

We're more than just cos-
Metically enhanced folk.
We're designed and loved.

Divine Images.
Not fashioned after monkeys.
Chips off the Old Block.

Hope

Theme: a reading about the nature of hope

A smile.

A moment of recognition.

A word of encouragement.

A pointing towards something more.

Something above.

Something beyond.

A reason to go on.

A reason to take another step.

Purpose at the crossroads.

Direction in the dark.

A port in the storm.

A man on a darkened hillside, pinned onto a backdrop of hate.

A sign of hope on a Sunday morning.

An impossible dream realised.

A fresh breath in a tomb.

A new set of footprints leaving a graveyard.

A promise.

A presence with us forever.

The Parable Of The Mustard Weed

Themes: The parable of the mustard seed
Bible Refs: Matthew 13 vv 31-32

Apparently mustard was a weed in Jesus's day, which turns his parable upside-down. Imagine Jesus saying, 'The kingdom of God is like bindweed…'

Till recently I looked up into the sky of my mind
And viewed a tree of huge proportions
Heard a story by a man from Nazareth
And imagined an ivory tower, a church so high
The idea filled my mind with grandeur
A bastion, a castle in the sky
Invulnerable, gleaming,
Perhaps even impenetrable
To those not in the know, those not in the crowd
Impressive birds come to nest
And make it their home
This mighty, magnificent mustard tree.

But I took a walk and overheard another story
About the smallest seed, so despised
Nothing epic or gleaming about this planting
No towering tree
Calling to the privileged birds of society
But an unwanted rejected weed

Not what I expected at all
Not what I thought it should be
A kingdom growing subversively
Unexpectedly spreading
Taking hold in the dark places
And yes, birds finding a place
But not an elevated one
Not a place of power
But alongside a rejected gardener
That man from Nazareth
Working close the ground
His kingdom resembling the kind of plant
I might normally

…reject.

Four Easter Monologues by Simon Peter

Originally broadcast Easter 2011 on Premier Christian Radio.

The first Easter, seen through the eyes of Peter
Bible Refs: Mark 14-16

1. Thursday Midnight

We'd been in hiding for a while. Cooped up in Bethany. Frankly I was getting bored, and the others were getting restless. We were holed up with the sisters of mercy as I call them, Martha and Mary. Mary's all right but Martha's just a nightmare, hyperactive or what? A little bit on the obsessive compulsive side if you ask me. Especially after Lazarus came back, not from being on holiday, from being dead. He'd been to Hades not Ibiza. Everyone was talking about it, so there'd been threats on his life. The word on the street was there was a fat reward out for anyone who bumped him off. (Add that to the death threats out on Jesus and you can imagine we were having a whale of a time.) Don't know what they were bothering for – didn't they get the point – he'd already been dead. Been there done that. Not much of a threat. Anyway, we were all hiding with the three of them, there'd been a lot of revolutionary talk in the streets after all that malarkey when Jesus rode into Jerusalem on the donkey, so Jesus was keeping his head well down for a while. Keeping out of trouble. Personally I think he missed a chance, he had the crowd eating out of his hand, you could see the authorities were well worried, and what did he do? Nothing. Just rode into town and rode out again. Some revolution.

Anyway you can't hide forever can you? Especially not with Martha and Mary and all the beggars they look after. So we badgered him about the Passover, it was party time, surely he wasn't hoping to celebrate the feast with the sisters of mercy.

Well he wasn't – he'd set up this secret meeting for us, somewhere the authorities and the stinking Romans wouldn't find us. It was all nudge nudge wink wink say no more. John and me slips into town looking for a man with water on his head. Fairly unusual in a city where it's woman's work. But we saw him and followed him and said all the right words, and frankly felt a bit stupid, but hey, it was all set up. We had a secret room prepared and the food was laid on.

So we're there, lapping it up, music, wine, food it was great. We were all having a fantastic time. Then he has to go and spoil it by keeping on about how he's gonna die soon. I tried to shut him up. I told him he wasn't even ill, and if anyone came looking for him we'd sort them. We'd spark a revolution no problem. I noticed Jude sat up when I said that. And right away Jesus nods at Jude and says, 'Hurry up, go and do it now,' so we figured bingo! Jude and Jesus have something cooking here. Things were looking up. Good job I brought my sword I thought..

'I'll die with you Jesus,' I said then, 'I'm not scared. Come on it's time we kicked out these Romans and brought in the kingdom of God.'

'No,' says Jesus. 'you can't come with me where I'm going at the moment.'

And I was like, what? 'Course we can, we'll follow you anywhere.'

'No you won't you'll run away all of you,' he says, and his face was as a grave as a tombstone. But he said, and then his face brightened, 'Don't worry. I'm coming back for you. I'm going to do something that will be like making a new LIFE for you. And you won't find me for a while. Then you'll see me.'

'What is this – hide and seek? See me – not see me.'

'No Peter,' says Jesus, 'it's life and death. It's not a game.'

Well that ruined the party good and proper. Jesus said something about us knowing where he was going and good old Tom pipes up and says, 'Like how? We haven't got a clue what you're talking about.'

Well, I lost the plot after that. We followed him outside to the olive grove, Judas turns up with a bunch of temple guards, there was madness in the dark, I lashed out and slashed one of the bad guys and then Jesus went and spoilt it by healing him. Sometimes I wonder whose side he's on.

And here I am now, hiding in the dark, waiting for Judas to let me in to this courtyard, 'cause this is where they've brought Jesus, arrested him and dragged him here. But it ain't over, when I'm inside I'll start a distraction and Jesus'll bring all heaven down on the place. Just like he did in the temple. They think it's over, they think they've won, but he hasn't even begun yet. You watch. Let battle commence.

- - - -

2. Friday Lunchtime

You know, three years can fly by can't it? Go like that. (snaps fingers)

One minute you're working by the water, the next you're walking on it. Last year I saw a blind man set free, last night I saw a seeing man get kidnapped. And not just any seeing man, a man who could see like no one ever saw before. That's what I can't understand. I've seen Messiahs rise and fall, but no one like him. No one with the insight and the humour and the authority.

Messiahs get crucified all the time around here. But you see it happen and you know – they wasn't the Messiah after all. Just the end of another era. More disappointment. And that's what I can't get through my head. If he wasn't the Messiah then how did he do it? How did he work all those miracles and come up with all those stories and that clever stuff that floored the Pharisees? How did he stay so calm, so compassionate? How did he not give up when he saw thousands of people stomp off badmouthing him after he took the trouble to feed them all.

I'll be honest, I'm disappointed. I really am. I mean, he promised me stuff. He made bold statements about freedom from oppression, peace on earth and all that. That's what everyone said was written in the sky the day he was born – peace on earth. Well where's the peace now. It was all a sham. I mean I've made mistakes, we've all made 'em. But I've learnt from them. The whole walking on water thing and sinking like a stone and the jokes that followed. 'Yea

Peter that's why you're the rock – 'cause you sink like one.' And the misunderstanding that time when I tried to help him and he got me confused with Satan... and when we went up that mountain and he did an impression of a... what? An angel? And I wanted to put up tents and stay up there forever... and when he did the miracle with the fish and it scared me stupid and I fell on my knees quaking like a little girl... anyway I admit it. I made my mistakes. But nothing like the mistake he's made. He promised us something more. He promised us on his life. He dared to give us hope. You don't do that to people who've lived their whole life under the fist of the Romans. That's not fair. That's criminal. He waxed about freedom and justice and a break from the oppression of those sick murderous Romans. And where's it got us? What's it all worth now? Nothing. He didn't even have the strength to argue his case with Pilate or Herod, didn't even call down at them from the cross when they spat and laughed at his pain. He was so weak. You don't change the world like that. Not by turning into some kind of meek lamb, being kicked about. Power, that's what beats your enemies. It's the only language they understand. Dying like a criminal will get you nowhere. A cold stone body, mutilated and rotting, that'll do nothing for Israel and the kingdom of God. Failure. That's all it was, and

I've just wasted the last three years of my life. Thank you very much. And before you start this is not about what happened in the courtyard. I know what you're thinking, I'm mad at him because I can't face myself. This has nothing to do with it. You'd have done the same. I mean what was I supposed to say? What good would it have done to admit I was on his side. He was going down. It was all over, me dying too, what good would that be? I signed up for something else. I know I said I'd die but I meant in battle, I meant in fighting for the cause, not in skulking in the dark being accused by some two-bit woman and a couple of drunk soldiers. I wasn't gonna go down like that. You'd have done the same. It's all lost. There was no gain in standing up and being counted. It wasn't my fault that I lied, it wasn't even lying. I was trying to collect something useful out of the wreckage of last night.

I know what it looks like, I know they'll be talking about Peter the rock sinking like one again, swearing he'd walk on water and then go through fire and then falling on his face at the first sign of trouble. Let 'em talk. They don't understand. They don't know me. They weren't even there. You weren't even there, so don't judge me, you weren't standing in the courtyard surrounded by enemies watching your dreams go down the pan. You weren't there.

- - - -

3. Saturday Evening

I heard he's been looking for me all day. Little John. Jesus's best mate. James's little brother. Right pain in the... I mean he always preferred James and John over me and Andrew. I never understood that. Andrew's like Mr Nice Guy – do anything for ya – them two they're like the Krays, with their demon mother hanging around in the background half the time. Oh great. No doubt he wants to chivvy me up, tell me everything'll be all right.

I heard something else too. About Judas. They say he's dead. Hanged himself. Went out in some field somewhere and threw a rope on some rotten old tree, fell and spilled his guts. It's crazy, we're all falling apart. Why'd he go and do that? Tom's gone awol, Matt's already planning to go back in business, Nathaniel and Philip and Simon are talking about switching to Jesus's brother James. It's always the way, if the Messiah gets bumped off then look to the family. Who's next in line? Well must be James, next one down. Though I can't see it myself. I think the Messiah gene skipped a generation when it comes to him. He's not leader material. He reckoned Jesus was mad. Tried to have him carted off a couple of times. How can he be the logical replacement. He's probably in with the Romans. The whole family are nuts if you ask me. They all reckoned Jesus should be locked up. What's the old saying? You can pick your friends but you're stuck with your family.

I hate myself. I was so naïve. So stupid. What an idiot. Thought I could be somebody.

- - - -

4. Sunday Morning

There's panic in the city, corpses everywhere. It's as if whatever Lazarus had was catching. The dawn of the dead has hit us. There was an earthquake early this morning, they found a load of open graves and now people who we'd thought long gone are back for good. Nathaniel's dead worried, his mother-in-law died last year and he's terrified she'll be back looking for him.

I don't know what to make of it. I know what you're thinking. It's this Jesus thing, there very strong rumours kicking around that he's back. In spite of many people watching him die writhing in agony very publically just a couple of days ago, suddenly they say he's breathing again, and more than breathing, talking, laughing, eating… and worst of all – looking for me. And if that's true I know what it's about. The courtyard. Me denying I ever knew him. Me saying I was gonna be a hero and then turning out like a loser instead.

Those women… You can't shut 'em up. Mary especially. They've seen him apparently. All of them. Alive and kicking. Which is fine but what's that count for? It won't stand up in court. He might as well have appeared to a talking donkey. Which he probably has done knowing him. Those women, they're driving me nuts. They say he can't wait to see me. They say he's been asking for me. Well, he'll have to come looking. I mean it wasn't as if I didn't give him the opportunity. I went, I looked. They weren't lying. The tomb was open. Something shook that rock free. He'd left his grave clothes behind, which I guess means he must have found something else to wear. But the point is – alive or dead, he wasn't there. Little John wouldn't go in but I wasn't spooked, don't know if he expected Jesus to suddenly leap out of the shadows with a quick 'Hey! I'm back.' But he didn't. Just the empty clothes. I don't know what's going on and I'm not alone. The others don't believe it, especially Thomas, and he's no fool.

Apparently, if the stories are to be believed, Mary and Jesus had quite a cosy little chat. Apparently he wanted to know – where were we all? That's what he said. 'Where were you all? There was no one waiting at the tomb. So disappointing. I told you I was coming back.' Don't know if he was expecting a welcome back party. All wine and free fish. Mary keeps going on about how 'it's the best feelgood ending in the history of feelgood endings'. I don't know what she means, doesn't feel good to me at all. I heard that a couple of the guys are planning on getting out. They think the stories of resurrection will just kick up an even greater storm for those of us left. The sheep dung'll really hit the flour grinder. The Romans will probably interpret these kinds of shenanigans as insurrection. We could all end up on crosses. So Cleopas is definitely on the run. He's packing for Emmaus even as I speak. I think I'll just go back to fishing. Who did I think I was anyway? I'm not Rabbi material. Jesus picked the wrong man here. I belong on the water. And I'm not talking about walking on it either – in a boat. That's what makes sense to me, fishing for people was a nice idea but that's enough of that.

Just so long as he doesn't go away again we'll be all right…

Not Fair (sketch and story versions)

Themes: The parable of the workers, God's mercy, God's ways
Bible Refs: Matthew 20 vv 1-15, Matthew 7 v 24 and Luke 23 vv 39-43

Similar to the **Not Fair** story on page 39, this could be performed as a group sketch, following the stage directions in italics. Or it could be told as a story with audience participation, teaching the responses highlighted in bold to everyone before beginning to tell the story.

Audience Responses:

£200 – all say "Whooo!" and look impressed
Foundation/s – All stamp feet twice & "Stamp!"
Contract - "Scribble scribble!"
Any kind of food – "Yum!" & rub stomachs
Mistake - Sharp breath & put hand to mouth

Once there was a woman who decided to build her own house. She knew nothing about building houses but she thought it couldn't be that difficult, so she bought a nice plot of land and started to dig.
Woman enters, waves hello, snaps fingers for idea, scratches head, shrugs, checks floor and then mimes digging

However, she made a big **mistake**, she built the house very quickly and on a swamp with no **foundations**.

And while she was asleep it collapsed and fell on top of her.

Build quickly, mime feet in swamp, fall asleep

She woke to find bits of the ceiling in her mouth and the toilet nowhere in sight.

Pick bits out of mouth and spit, then cross legs for loo

So she decided to try again, this time she bought a bit of land that was good and solid, and this time she decided to get some help.

Check land and snap fingers for an idea

So she went into the nearby town and found some people sitting around on the bench outside the job centre.

A group enter and lean on each other

The woman sees the group

'I want some help to build my house,' she said.

'I want some help to build my house.'

'I want it done properly with good **foundations**'

*'I want it done properly with good **foundations**'*

'and a nice little fountain in the garden.'

'and a nice little fountain in the garden.'

But the people said they were too busy having a rest.

'We're too busy having a rest.'

So she scratched her head, had a think and then said, 'I'll pay you all £200 if you'll help me.'

'I'll pay you all £200 if you'll help me.'

Suddenly – they weren't so busy, and they leapt up, signed a **contract** and started work on the house.

All look wide-eyed. All leap up and sign a contract and shake the woman's hand, dig and turn backs

At coffee time she went into town to buy some **doughnuts** for everyone and she spotted a large group of people on the bench outside the job centre. She asked them if they wanted to earn a few quid.

'Want to earn a few quid?'

They all leapt up and she had to buy twice as many **doughnuts**.

Sign contract

At lunchtime the woman went into town to buy some **veggie burgers**. She spotted some more people outside the job centre. She asked them if they wanted to help him build a house.

'Want to help me build a house?'

And so they leapt up and helped him carry the **veggie burgers** back to the building site.

Sign contract and carry burgers

At teatime she went in for some **cream cakes** and saw another crowd. So she asked them if they wanted to help her as well.

'Do you want to help me as well?' All leap up

By the time they'd finished work the building site was full of weary workers and empty food bags.

All finish work and look tired

The woman said, 'Come and collect your wages.'

'Come and collect your wages.'

The teatime recruits lined up first and the woman paid them each **£200**.

Line up. Woman walks down line and pays them

'Excellent!' said the lunchtime recruits, 'we'll get twice as much.'

They rub their hands and turn away

'Cool!' said the coffee time recruits. 'We'll get three times as much!'

They turn back, stick thumbs up and turn away

'Even better,' said the morning recruits, 'we'll get four times as much.'

They turn back, and punch the air

But they didn't, they all got **£200**. There was nearly a riot.

Woman pays them. All look horrified and angry

'Grrr!' they said.

'Grrrr!'

'It's not fair,' they said. 'We've worked all day and only got the same as the people who just did a bit at the end.'

They all jab their palms

'Oh dear,' said the woman, 'I must have made a **mistake**.'

'Oh dear, I must have made a mistake.'

She said and she scratched her head and looked confused.

The woman scratches her head and looks confused

So the woman took out their **contracts** and had a

look.

The woman does this, they all gather round behind him, looking over her shoulder

'No, that's right,' she said. 'Look, you agreed to work all day for **£200**. It says so here.'

She points this out on the form, they all look and frown

'Yes, but that's not fair...' they said.

'Yes, but that's not fair...'

But the woman shook her head and said:

*'There's no **mistake**. It's my money, if I want to be generous that's up to me. There's no need for you to get stingy about it.'*

All freeze then walk off.

Carry On Spying?

Themes: Joshua sends out two spies
Bible Refs: Joshua 2 v 1

Ten spies walk on and stand in a line. Joshua joins them and looks them up and down.

Josh. Right you lot – you've been recommended to me as the best secret agents we have. Is that right? Are you tough?

All. (Loudly, with enthusiasm) Sir!

Josh. Are you brave?

All. Sir!

Josh. Do you wanna be James Bond?

All. Sir!

Josh. Are you willing to die?

All. S... er... (scratch heads)

Josh. Hmm. Okay, listen up. We're looking for some spies to send into the promised land.

All. Sir!

Josh. 40 years ago we sent twelve of our top agents into the promised land. Hands up all those who went in on that first mission.

(Spies 1 and 2 put their hands up)

Josh. Are you sure?

Sp 1. Er... well....

Sp 2. What was the question again?

Josh.   I said, hands up all those who went on the first mission.

(No hands go up.)

Josh.   Exactly. There's only me and Caleb left. You know why? You know what finished them off?

Sp 3. Bird flu?

Josh.   Nope.

Sp 4. Man-flu?

Josh.   Nope.

Sp 5   Mad cow disease?

Josh.   Nope. It was fear. They were scared.

Sp 6. Huh! Well we'll never get killed. We're not scared. They were obviously rubbish spies. So who got 'em in the end?

Josh.   God.

Sp 6. Ah! Scary!

Josh.   Yes. You see – we have orders – from God.

All.   Sir!

Josh.   We've been instructed to light up the world like stars!

Sp 4. Superstars?

Josh.   No – just – ordinary stars. Nice and bright. But those spies went into the Promised Land and all they saw was the problems. Whereas me and Caleb – we saw grapes as big as the sun. We saw milk and honey flowing like rivers. We saw big huge chocolate fountains and mountains of marshmallows and doughnuts as big as the O2. It looked like the Garden of Eden all over again. So – do you want to go back to Eden?

All. Sir!

Josh. Even if it's very, very, very, very scary?

All. Er…

Josh. Think of those marshmallow mountains.

All. Sir!

Josh. Well I need two spies who will find a way in for us.

Sp 1. Only two, sir?

Josh. Yep. Last time twelve went in and only
two of us were any good. So I thought we'd forget about the other ten. This is not a mission to see how good paradise is – this is a mission to find our way back in. Who's up for it?

All. (salute) Sir! (and then step forward)

Josh. You might get killed. (all hands go down and they all step back)

All. You go. No you go. You're his favourite. I am not. He likes you! No he doesn't! You're brave. I'm not! (they try to push each other to volunteer)

Josh. All right. Everyone think of a number. (Pause) Right! Time's up! What numbers did you think of?

Sp 1. Er…20.

Sp 2. 30.

Sp 3. 40.

Sp 4. 100!

Sp 5. 200!

Sp 6. 500!

Sp 7. 800!

Sp 8. 1000!

Sp 9. A million.

Sp 10. A million… and one!

Josh. Right then – you two can go.

Sp 10. What? But we picked the biggest – they only picked like twenty!

Josh. Yep – and I decided that whoever picked the two biggest numbers would go.

Sp 10. But you didn't tell us – that's not fair!

Josh. Too late. Off you go.

(They all start to leave the same way. Joshua stops Spies 9 and 10)

Josh. Oi! The promised land's that way. (He points in the opposite direction)

Spies 9 & 10 leave in the other direction, sighing and shaking their heads.

The Antenatal Class

Themes: Various biblical mums-to-be meet
Bible Refs: Joshua 2, Genesis 38, Ruth 1-4, 2 Samuel 11, Genesis 19, Genesis 29, Genesis 21, Luke 1 & 2

A line of heavily pregnant mothers walk on and stand in a semi-circle, including – Mary, Rahab, Sarah, Lot's daughters [LD 1&2], Ruth, Bathsheba, Leah & Tamar, & the group leader.

Lead. Welcome everyone to your first antenatal class. Perhaps, as this is the first meeting we could all go round and say a bit about ourselves. Rahab – would you like to start?

Rah. All right. My name's Rahab, I live in Jericho and I'm having a boy.

Lead. And what do you do for a living?

Rah. Er... I'm a (speaks into her hand as if coughing)

Lead. Sorry?

Rah. I'm a prostitute.

Lead. (shocked) Oh! (pause) Does it pay well? (Rahab holds up both hands, she is wearing a load of expensive rings. Others look at each other, and whisper to each other and nod towards her.)

Lead. Well, er… lovely. Moving on. (indicates to Tamar)

Tam. My name's Tamar, I'm from Canaan. And I'm having a boy.

Lead. (smiles) And I suppose you're not a… (whispers in Tamar's ear)

Tam. No but I did pretend to be one to get pregnant.

Lead. What!! Right! Moving quickly on… (indicates to Ruth)

Ruth. My name's Ruth, I'm from Moab, and…

Lead. From Moab?

Ruth. Yes.

Lead. You're a long way from home.

Ruth. I came with my mother-in-law. She was on her own, she lost everything she had.

Lead. That's very sad.

Ruth. Yes. We had nothing for a long time, we were just refugees, but now things are better, I have a new husband and a new baby.

Bath. And My name's Bathsheba and I'm from…

Lead. Oh yes, we've all heard of you.

Bath. What d'you mean?

Lead. You're married to the famous king. David the man God chose.

LD1. Ooh – he's good looking.

LD2. And rich!

Ruth. Yes, and he's kind and strong.

Tam. He's a good man, tell us about him.

Bath. He killed my husband.

All. What!

Lead. Er… Leah? Would you like to… talk. Now! Quickly!

Leah. My name's Leah, I'm married to Jacob. He got married to me by mistake.

Lead. By mistake?

Leah. Yes, he thought he was marrying my sister.

Lead. Oh! Was he in the same room as you when you got married? How far away from each other were you exactly?

Leah. Not far. I was wearing a veil.

Lead. A veil?

Leah. Yes. A very very very very thick veil. It was a sort of April fool trick. Anyway – Sarah over there is my great aunt.

Lead. Really? Your great aunt? How old are you, if you don't mind me asking?

Sarah. 90.

Lead. (shocked!) 90!! Wow! That is… great! And you're pregnant? Well er… well… well… well done you! And you two – do you come from a nice part of the world?

LD 1. Sodom.

Lead. I beg your pardon?

LD1. We come from Sodom.

LD2. But we've moved away now.

Lead. Really? I'm not surprised, it's not the nicest of places to bring up a baby.

LD2. Oh it wasn't that – God blew it up.

Lead. Oh!

LD1. Yea we had to leave before we got melted by fire and brimstone.

Lead. Rrrrright – ever think about going back?

LD2. It would be difficult – God wiped it off the face of the earth.

Lead. What does your mum feel about that?

LD1. Not a lot – she's a pile of salt.

LD2. We keep her in the kitchen cupboard.

Lead. (forces a smile) I think we'll move on.

Mar. I'm Mary.

(All the mums grab their stomachs and look surprised.)

Lead. Ah. Right. Your baby's very special. You've been given a child that will change the world.

LD1. What about our babies?

Lead. Oh yes, they're all special – but I have a feeling your children will pave the way for this one. They will set the scene for the greatest baby of all.

(They all pause and look puzzled, frown and look each other.)

Rah. Can we have the tea and biscuits now?

Tam. Yea I'm starving.

Ruth. How about a banana and marmite sandwich?

All.   Ooh yes!

Mar.   With some bacon and peanut butter.

Lead. (with a smile) Good idea. Come this way.

They all leave, chatting to each other about various strange food combinations.

Hidden Extras (i.e. not found in the index)

The Snake Drops By

 Now the serpent was the shrewdest of all the creatures that God had made. He slipped up to the woman in a quiet moment one morning and whispered, 'Really?'

'Really what?' she said.

'Did God really say you must not eat any of the fruit in the garden?' the snake hissed.

She laughed. 'Of course we may eat it,' the woman told him. 'It's only the fruit from the tree at the centre of the garden that we're not allowed to eat. God says we mustn't eat it or even touch it, or we'll die.'

'Hmm,' the snake pondered this for a moment. 'Tell you what then,' he said, 'have one of these instead.'

'What is it' the woman asked.

'Oh don't worry, it's not off that tree you don't like. It'll be really useful. Honest.'

She reached out and took the object,. Turned it in her fingers. It shone in the sunlight and made a bright ticking sound. 'Interesting,' she said.

'It is yes, you keep it? Okay?'

She smiled and nodded and examined the object more closely. She liked the detail and the carefully crafted digits on the front of it.

As the snake slithered away he looked back one more time and called, 'Oh I forgot to say, it'll also make you worry about the past, fret about the future, argue about arriving and leaving, stress about your journeying, clash about working, generally make you miserable and help you miss the present moment. Enjoy.'

The woman sat there staring after the snake, wondering what he meant by the past, present and future. Eventually she laid the clock down beside her in the dust, wondering if she'd ever find a use for it.

A Tale of Two Fathers

A mime for a group of two-eight people and one narrator. Draws on The Prodigal Son in Luke 15.

Narrator (pause between each line as the group freezes in the described poses):

The good father brings up his children with care
Each person in the group mimes holding a baby
He is patient and kind to them
Carefully place the child in a cot
He provides for them
Mime picking up a rattle and shaking it, then place it in the cot
He protects and watches over them
Place hands on side of cot and look over at the child

The bad father doesn't
Step back and sneer
He is selfish and rude
Mime shouting at the child
He mistreats them
Raise hand as if to slap
And he abandons them when they need him most
Turn away

The good father doesn't
Turn back and see older child, bend down to them

He listens
Smile and listen to them
And communicates
Mime talking, shaking and nodding head
Instructs and encourages them on
Freeze in a cheering pose

PAUSE

One father gave all he could to his son
Pull money from pockets and hold it out
And then watched him walk away
Watch sadly and wave goodbye
And waste it all
Look horrified
Was he angry?
Angry expression
Was he resentful?
Sneer, and throw up hands
Did he reject the boy?
Hold out hand to push away and then turn away
No
Turn and look at the narrator, surprised
When his son came back, having lost everything, he welcomed him and threw a welcome home party
Look, hand above eyes, look amazed and happy, and throw arms open wide, shout out loud, 'My son!'

All freeze.

Walking the Garden

God took a walk in the garden
Found a couple of lonely lost souls
Not so long ago they'd been happy
Now they shivered, but not from the cold.

There was warmth in the evening air
But frost buried deep in their eyes
Where once there had been truth and light
There was now the glimmer of lies.

They had nothing to hide from each other
Till they met a sweet talking snake
Now they need help to be honest
Now their smile is a little bit fake.

So God skins an innocent animal
The first death of many to come
Sheds blood to cover their shame
One day it will be his son…

Sacrificed for everyone's shame
A cover for everyone's loss
What began with those two in the garden
Will eventually lead to a cross.

And death at the hands of tyrants
As cynical hatred burns
But their world will shatter and shake
When the sacrificed son returns.

And so God keeps walking the garden
For people who want to break free
To escape the hiding and fakery
To get back to reality.

Made in the USA
Columbia, SC
31 August 2017